DISCARD

0000100125387

Living in
Victorian
Times

Sydney Wood

Senior lecturer in history,
Aberdeen College of Education

JOHN MURRAY

A note on money

In Victorian times people used money that was a little different from ours: pounds, shillings and pence (or pennies).

Twenty shillings made up a pound.
Twelve pennies made up a shilling.

The money was shown in figures like this:

One penny was written as 1d.
One shilling was written as 1s or 1/-.
One shilling and six pence was written as 1s 6d or 1/6.

Pounds, shillings and pence were all worth a very great deal more than they are today. A Victorian worker who earned £100 a year would think himself quite well paid.

A note on spelling

Some spellings have been modernised to make the text clearer.

© Sydney Wood 1985

First published 1985
by John Murray (Publishers) Ltd
50 Albemarle Street, London W1X 4BD

All rights reserved
Unauthorised duplication
contravenes applicable laws

Set by Fakenham Photosetting Ltd,
Fakenham, Norfolk
Printed and bound in Great Britain
at the Pitman Press, Bath

British Library Cataloguing in Publication Data

Wood, Sydney
   Living in Victorian times.
   1. Great Britain—Social conditions—19th century
   I. Title
   941.081   HN385

ISBN 0–7195–4120–4

Contents

1 Queen Victoria at the age of twenty

Introduction: The Age of Victoria

The new Queen

In 1837 Princess Victoria was eighteen years old. She was rather small—about five feet in height—and plump. Her uncle, King William IV, seldom saw his niece. Victoria lived with her mother, the Duchess of Kent. The Duchess had a fierce temper and had quarrelled with the King. The Princess lived a quiet life, though she very much enjoyed dancing, singing and riding. In 1837 this quiet life changed. The King had no children of his own; Victoria was the heir to the Crown.

Victoria often ended important days by writing down what had happened to her. This is how she described the way 20 June 1837 began.

> I was awoke at six o'clock by Mamma who told me that the Archbishop of Canterbury and Lord Conyngham were here and wished to see me. I got out of bed and went into my sitting room (only in my dressing gown) and alone and saw them, Lord Conyngham then acquainted me that my poor Uncle the King was no more and had expired at twelve minutes past twelve this morning and that consequently I am Queen. I am very young and perhaps in many, though not in all things, inexperienced, but I am sure that very few have more real good will and more real desire to do what is fit and right than I have.
>
> A. C. Benson and Viscount Esher (eds),
> *Letters of Queen Victoria*, 1905

Victoria and Albert

Victoria moved into Buckingham Palace. She placed her quarrelsome mother in rooms at the far end of the very large palace! Yet she very much needed someone to guide and advise her. Her Uncle Leopold, the King of the Belgians, urged her to marry as soon as possible. He even went so far as to suggest a husband for her. He urged Victoria to marry Prince Albert who came from the tiny German state of Saxe-Coburg. The anxious Queen Victoria wrote to her uncle,

> Though all the reports of Albert are most favourable and though I have little doubt I shall like him, still one can never answer beforehand for feelings and I may not have the feeling for him which is requisite to ensure happiness.

But when Victoria met the Prince, all her doubts were swept away. Albert was very ready to marry the Queen of a rich and powerful country. Victoria adored him. She wrote to the delighted Leopold,

> My mind is quite made up and I told Albert this morning of it: the warm affection he showed me on learning this gave me great pleasure. He seems perfection and I think that I have the prospect of very great happiness before me. I love him more than I can say. My feelings are a little changed I must say since last Spring when I said I couldn't think of marrying for three or four years; but seeing Albert has changed all this.

The royal marriage lasted from 1840 until the Prince's death in 1861. During these years the Queen gave birth to nine children. After the birth of the first child, Leopold wrote to Victoria to say that he hoped she would have many children. Victoria sent back this sharp reply.

2 The Queen and Prince Albert arrive for the opening of the Great Exhibition

> Men never think, at least seldom think, what a hard task it is for us women to go through this very often. God's will be done, and if he decrees that we are to have a great number

of children, why we must try to bring them up as useful and exemplary members of society.

The Queen agreed to take chloroform to ease the pain of the birth of her eighth child. This helped to make the use of chloroform more popular.

Albert was a very serious and hard-working man. He helped the Queen with all her duties—indeed Victoria believed he was better suited to royal duties than she was. She wrote,

Albert grows daily fonder and fonder of politics and business and is so wonderfully fit for both—such perspicacity [wisdom] and such courage—and I grow daily to dislike them more and more. We women are not made for governing and if we are good women we must dislike these masculine occupations.

The Great Exhibition of 1851 was one of the most successful of the Prince's schemes. A huge glass building called the Crystal Palace was built in Hyde Park. The organisers placed inside it objects from Britain and from all over the world. There were works of art, modern machines, and countless things made by machines and by craftsmen. The Queen was delighted with the opening of the Exhibition and wrote afterwards,

The waving palms, flowers, statues, myriads [large numbers] of people filling the galleries and seats around, the flourish of trumpets as we entered, gave us a sensation which I can never forget and I felt much moved. God bless my dearest Albert, God bless my dearest country which has shown itself so great today.

The Queen never really recovered from the shock of Albert's death in 1861. Not long afterwards she wrote to her Uncle Leopold,

My life as a happy one is ended. The world is gone for me! If I must live on it is henceforth for our poor fatherless children—for my unhappy country which has lost all in losing him—and in only doing what I know and feel he would wish, for he is near me—his spirit will guide and inspire me.

The Queen's later years

Victoria withdrew from important events; for many years after Albert's death the public rarely saw her. She spent a lot of her time in Scotland. There she lived at Balmoral Castle, which Albert had helped to design. She went for carriage and pony rides, she walked and sketched. She went on journeys to other

3 Balmoral Castle

lonely parts of Scotland and wrote about her travels. This description comes from a journey she made to Western Scotland.

> Ben Lomond, blue and yellow, rose above the lower hills which were pink and purple with heather. We got out and sketched. Only here and there were some poor little cottages with picturesque barefooted lasses and children to be seen. There was no crowd, no trouble or annoyance, and during the whole of our drive nothing could be quieter or more agreeable. Hardly a creature did we meet. This solitude, the romance and wild loneliness of everything here, the absence of hotels and beggars, the independent simple people who all speak Gaelic here, all make beloved Scotland the proudest finest country in the world.

Victoria gradually began to return to public life. In 1897 she celebrated sixty years as Queen. This Diamond Jubilee was a

4

4 *Queen Victoria on the day of her Diamond Jubilee*

time of great rejoicing. A little choirboy who went up from Windsor to St Paul's has left us this description of what happened.

> Oh, it was a sight that we saw. The roads were all lined with Jack tars [sailors] and soldiers. The Queen was dressed in black with silver on it. She had a black bonnet made of lace trimmed with white flowers. She carried a white lace sunshade and she had a fan. Her parasol was up. The Queen looked very well indeed and ever so happy. Everybody looked very well. On the other hand lots of people fainted in the crowds. Sir George Martin conducted and all the people joined in the singing. After the National Anthem the Archbishop of Canterbury called out 'Three cheers for the Queen'.
>
> After all this the procession moved away and left us in peace to eat our dinner on the lawn in front of St. Paul's. It seemed funny to eat in a churchyard but we were hungry all the same and the graves didn't spoil our appetites one bit.
>
> R. Thorndike, *Children of the Garter*, 1937

Victoria died in 1901. She had been Queen for sixty-three and a half years. Her subjects rarely saw her and she had no real idea of how most ordinary people lived.

The following chapters explore the lives of the Queen's subjects through the words that they themselves wrote, the pictures they drew and the photographs they took.

1 Write a short newspaper report with the headline 'Our New Queen'. Describe what Victoria looked like and what sort of person she seemed to be.

2 Why did Victoria think that Albert was better at carrying out royal duties than she was? Do you agree with her? Give a reason for your answer.

3 Look at what Victoria wrote about Scotland. Suggest two reasons why the Queen liked to spend so much time there after Albert's death.

4 Are the lives of our royal family today different from Victoria's? Are they able to spend most of their time out of the public's eye?

1　The Rich

Britain in the age of Queen Victoria was one of the world's richest countries. It led the world in building up big industries that produced great quantities of goods to be sold all over the world. British ships sailed the oceans carrying much of the world's trade. British skills, British money and British workers built railways in many countries. As a result of all this activity the number of rich people increased. A man who earned more than £1,000 a year was able to afford a very comfortable life. He and his family could live in a large house with several servants. Some men earned far more than this and owned several houses. As well as the growing number of rich men who had made their money in business, there were the wealthy landowners of the upper classes and the aristocracy.

The aristocracy included some odd people. The Earl of Bridgewater, for instance, gave dinner parties for his dogs. The animals were dressed in men's or women's clothes and sat at the table with napkins tucked under their chins, while servants

5 Waddesdon Manor, near Aylesbury

brought their food. Such wealthy people usually owned a large country house and a big house in a fashionable part of London.

A man who earned around £350 to £1,000 a year was quite well off. Although he just had one home, he could afford to pay for two or three servants to wait upon himself and his family.

Rich men did not expect their wives and daughters to work. While the men spent their time in their factories, offices, shops, or on political and legal matters, wealthy women had little to do.

Women tried to make the homes where they spent so much time as comfortable as possible. A French lady called Flora Tristan, who came to London in 1839, was horrified to see how little rich London women had to do. She wrote,

> I think I can guess what gives English ladies the title of housewives, it is their sedentary existence. They rise very late, dawdle over breakfast, read the newspapers and dress: at two there is another meal, then they read novels and write letters.
> J. Hawkes (ed.), *The London Journal of Flora Tristan*, 1842

This life was boring for some women. Florence Nightingale longed to take up nursing. She hated the empty hours of her time at home. In later life she looked back and remembered.

> Oh weary days—oh evenings that never seem to end—for how many years have I watched that drawing room clock and thought it would never reach ten, and for twenty, thirty years more to do this. I know nothing like the petty

6 A Victorian drawing room

grinding tyranny of a good English family.
Quoted in C. Woodham Smith, *Florence Nightingale*, 1950

Rich young women's lives were controlled by strict rules. They were not allowed to go out on their own. The Countess of Lovelace remembered these rules.

The well-guarded girl of the years 1870–80 could not walk alone in the street or drive alone in a cab or on a railway carriage. How many a long dull summer afternoon have I passed indoors because there was no room for me in the family carriage and no lady's maid who had time to walk out with me.
Quoted in A. Sproule, *The Social Calendar*, 1978

1 Look at Picture 6. List as many things as possible that show this is not a modern room.

7 *Upper-class young ladies out walking with a footman. Notice that he is carrying their books for them*

2   Look at Picture 7. What do you think the two young ladies might be saying to each other? Write a short imaginary conversation. They might mention how glad they are to be out and how they feel about not being allowed out alone.

The children of the rich

During her visit to London, Flora Tristan noticed that rich English families did not seem to take much interest in their young children. She explained,

> This is what happens in wealthy families: the children are confined to the third floor with their nurse; the mother asks for them when she wishes to see them and only then do the children come to pay her a short visit. When the nurse takes them down to her in the drawing room she looks to see that they are clean and have fresh clothes on, once she has finished her inspection she kisses them and that is all until tomorrow.
>
> *The London Journal of Flora Tristan*, 1842

8 The nursery at Minley Manor in Hampshire

Flora Tristan did not like the English and her opinions are very harsh. But rich children were usually brought up by servants, not by their parents. They had a nurse to care for them and a governess to teach them. Around the age of eight to ten boys were sent off to school (see Chapter 7) but girls were often given their lessons at home.

Winston Churchill wrote about his early childhood. He belonged to one of Britain's most important families. His father was a famous politician. He remembered that he was especially worried by the news that a governess was coming.

> I did what so many oppressed peoples have done in similar circumstances; I took to the woods. I hid in extensive shrubberies. Hours passed before I was retrieved and handed over to 'the Governess'. We continued to toil every day, not only at letters but at words, and also at what was much worse, figures.
>
> My mother took no part in these impositions, but she gave me to understand that she approved of them and she sided with the Governess almost always. My mother always seemed to me a fairy princess: a radiant being possessed of limitless riches and power. She shone for me like the Evening Star. I loved her dearly—but at a distance. My nurse was my confidante. Mrs Everest it was who looked after me and tended all my wants. It was to her I poured out my many troubles both now and in my schooldays.
>
> *My Early Life*, 1930

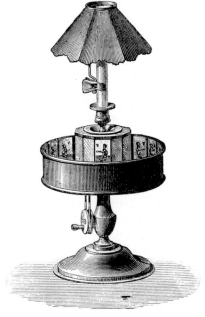

9 A zoetrope ('wheel of life'). The drum containing pictures is made to spin round and the figures in the pictures seem to move

The rich child's nursery was full of toys. Winston Churchill wrote, 'I had such wonderful toys: a real steam engine, a magic lantern and a collection of soldiers nearly a thousand strong.'

Toymakers in Victorian times were very skilful. They made toys that worked by clockwork and others that used sand or water to make the parts move.

Victorian families usually had five or six children. Many children, like Margaret Booth, had a busy, happy childhood. Margaret's father was Charles Booth, a rich shipowner. The family had a country home and a house in Kensington, London. When they were in London (Margaret wrote later)

> Children took walks with governesses, there were Monday 'pops' [popular concerts] and there were dinner parties. The gentlemen and ladies walked arm in arm down the stairs and small girls in white frocks watched them and listened for the buzz of conversation.

A man selling muffins walked by the house.

> It was thrilling to watch from our window the nurserymaid

run out to stop him and buy his wares. Nor must we leave out the organgrinder. How cheerfully he ground out tunes such as 'Will you be mine?'

On Sundays Margaret's father came up to the nursery and helped the children to colour in picture books.

Then everything must be cleared away and tea laid and if Maria our nurserymaid were in a good temper she would make 'Fizzledick', that is toast our slices of bread and butter by the fire. After tea there was my mother to read aloud and show picture books.

'Six to Sixteen at Gracedieu', in D. Crow,
Victorian Women, 1971

1 List three ways in which the children of the rich spent their time.
2 What do children do today that Victorian children would never have heard of?
3 How do you think a zoetrope worked?

Clothes

10 A Victorian corset

Rich Victorians owned a great many clothes. They needed to keep warm in the large rooms of their homes. Many big houses were cold and draughty, even though each room had its own coal fire. The rich showed off their wealth and their success by wearing expensive clothes. When a Victorian man dressed he first put on a vest and long-legged pants made of rough woollen material. What he wore next depended on what season of the year it was, what time of day it was, and what sort of work he was going to do. Quite strict rules existed about the correct clothes for certain times and certain events: the man who ignored them was likely to be ridiculed. Books were published to guide those who were not sure what to wear. One of them advised,

When you are in town you mustn't appear in a lounge suit and a bowler hat after lunch, and of course if you have any business appointment in the morning you would wear a frock or morning coat with a silk hat. In August and September society people are not supposed to be in town and therefore if you happen to be in town you can wear country clothes—a light lounge suit and a straw hat. If you are in town in August and September you are supposed to be there only because you are passing through on your way to the country. Don't wear tan boots or shoes with a black coat. Don't wear a silk hat when you are wearing a navy blue jacket. Of course no gentleman ever wears a made-up tie.

Clothes and the Man, by 'The Major of Today', 1900

Women's clothes were even more complicated. Rich women tried to make themselves seem as slim-waisted as possible by wearing corsets with laces that were pulled as tightly as possible. This is how one lady remembered Victorian clothes.

> The thought of the discomfort, restraint and pain which we had to endure from our clothes makes me even angrier now than it did then. Except for the most small-waisted, naturally dumb-bell shaped females, the ladies never seemed at ease. Their dresses were always made too tight. [Corsets] were real instruments of torture; they prevented me from breathing and dug deep holes into my softer parts on every side.
>
> Gwen Raverat, *Period Piece*, 1952

Rich women's clothes showed they did not need to work. During the 1850s and 1860s they wore very wide 'crinoline skirts'. A foreign visitor to Britain described crinoline wearers.

> They have a habit of puffing out their skirts from waist to hem by means of whalebone or even wire hoops. These

13

12 The bustle

skirts swing like bells and give their wearers a jerky gait [walk] which is not graceful.

Francis Wey, 1856, in A. Adburgham, *Shops and Shopping*, 1964

In the 1880s and 1890s crinolines went out of fashion. Instead fashionable women wore bustles. Their skirts were made to stick out a long way at the back by means of a large pad fastened below the waist. By 1900 Victorian women were wearing more practical clothes, but they still wore many layers.

1   Suggest two reasons why Victorian women wore so many clothes.
2   Imagine you are the man in charge of the bus in Picture 11. What do you mutter to yourself as you see this passenger approaching and have to help her on board?

Food

Rich Victorians were fond of their food. They were able to choose from a huge range of things to eat brought from all over the world. Food became cheaper during the nineteenth century. Before this it was usual for the rich to eat a large breakfast, a very substantial dinner at midday, an early evening meal and a late evening supper. The Victorians changed this arrangement.

14

They moved the evening meal to a later time, calling it 'dinner', and added afternoon tea to fill the long hours between their midday 'luncheon' and 'dinner', which was served around 7.30 or 8 p.m.

Victorians began their day with much bigger breakfasts than are common today. The recipe books of the time show what they ate. The most famous of these was written by Mrs Isabella Beeton. She found that people who were becoming rich were eager to buy her books in order to learn how they ought to behave. This is what she suggested for breakfast.

> Any cold meat the larder may furnish should be nicely garnished and be placed on the buffet. Potted meats or fish, cold game or poultry, veal and ham pies, game and rump steak pies are all suitable dishes for the breakfast table, also cold ham and tongue.
>
> The following list of hot dishes may perhaps assist our readers in knowing what to provide for the comfortable meal called breakfast. Boiled fish such as mackerel, whiting, herring etc., mutton chops and rump steaks, boiled sheep's kidneys, sausages, plain rashers of bacon, bacon

13 *A Victorian dinner party (1890)*

and poached eggs, ham and poached eggs, omelettes, muffins, toast etc.

Book of Household Management, 1861

Dinner was the most important meal. Victorians could display their wealth by serving huge meals and decorating their tables with expensive silver and glass. They dropped the earlier habit of placing many dishes on the table and letting guests pick and choose. At a Victorian dinner party each course was served separately. Menus were written in French. This letter, written in 1875 in Cambridge, shows that a reasonably well-off Victorian ate well.

I gave a dinner party on Thursday and left the preparation of the meal to [Mrs Bird the cook] simply giving my orders and everything was perfect. I got a girl in to help. First [Mrs Bird] made the rolls herself. Then she made white soup, she fried twelve fillets of sole and made the lobster sauce to go with the fish. Next we had two entrées, first 'timballes de foie gras' and then when this was eaten, sweetbreads stewed with mushrooms and truffles. Mrs Bird roasted the leg of mutton, boiled the turkey, made its sauce of oysters and cooked all the vegetables, potatoes, cauliflower and celery. When we were through with this she sent up the roast duck in its sauce. I hired two waiters to help Martin and everything passed off delightfully. We had a plum pudding and after that a Charlotte Russe, then cheese, and then the table was cleared for dessert. All the wine glasses, decanters etc. were taken off and then new decanters put on and dessert plates. The waiters then handed round one dish after another of the dessert after which we ladies arose and left the room to the gentlemen.

M. R. Bobbitt (ed.), *With Dearest Love to All: Letters of Lady Jebb*, 1960

When dinner ended the gentlemen stayed for some time on their own. They drank port and chatted before rejoining the ladies in the drawing room.

People also bought books to learn good manners. At dinner,

Soup should be eaten with a table spoon, not a dessert [in these days no one 'drank' soup: it was eaten]. Fish should be eaten with a silver fish knife and fork. Peas should be eaten with a fork. Jellies, blancmanges, iced puddings etc. should be eaten with a fork. When eating cheese small morsels should be placed with a knife on small morsels of bread and the two conveyed to the mouth with the thumb and finger. As a matter of course young ladies do not eat

cheese at dinner parties.
Manners and Rules of Good Society (anon.), 1888

Occasionally late evening parties took place. William Taylor was a footman in a wealthy house who served the guests at one of these gatherings. He wrote (making all sorts of mistakes in his English),

There is all kinds of sweet cakes and biscuits, lemonade, orangeade and many other pleasant drinks, but the best is the different kinds of ices. The company comes jenerally about ten or eleven. Sweet-hearting matches are very often made up at these parties. It is quite disgusting to a modest eye to see the way the young ladies dress to attract the notice of the gentlemen. They are nearly naked to the waist, only just a little bit of dress hanging on the shoulder. Plenty of false haire and teeth and paint.

William Taylor's diary, quoted in J. Burnett,
Useful Toil, 1974

1 Read about the dinner party cooked by Mrs Bird. Write it out as a menu to be put on the table in front of each guest. (You can see one of these little menus in Picture 13.)
2 Look at Picture 13. How many different wines are the guests going to drink? How can you work out the answer?
3 Imagine you have been a guest at an important Victorian dinner party. Write a letter to a friend describing everything that happened. Mention the clothes you wore, the people you met, the food you ate.

2 Life Below Stairs

Huge numbers of servants made life comfortable for the rich. During the nineteenth century Britain's population increased greatly and many boys and girls found it hard to get work. More and more of them became servants. By 1891 nearly a third of girls aged between fifteen and twenty worked as domestic servants. In 1871 the Earl of Leicester's country home of Holkham Hall was served by the following:

A valet to serve the Earl who was paid	£60 a year
A houseporter	£30 ,, ,,
A butler	£100 ,, ,,
Two footmen who were each paid	£32 ,, ,,
A steward's room boy who was paid	£18 ,, ,,
A female housekeeper	£40 ,, ,,
A cook	£60 ,, ,,
A lady's maid	£22 ,, ,,
A second lady's maid	£20 ,, ,,
Two kitchen-maids, one paid £18, the other	£10 ,, ,,
A scullery maid who was paid	£12 ,, ,,
A nurse	£36 ,, ,,
A nursemaid	£29 ,, ,,

Seven housemaids paid £20, £18, £16, £14, three at £12
Four laundry-maids at £22, £16, two at £10.
Two stillroom* maids paid at £16 and £12.

A. Hartcup, *Below Stairs in Great Country Houses*, 1980

The housekeeper and the butler were in charge of the servants. The rich families who paid the servants also provided rooms where they slept and often paid for uniforms too. The servants had to work long hours, seven days a week. They had to obey strict rules. These were some of the rules at Holkham Hall.

> Every servant is expected to be punctually in his/her place at the time of meals. Breakfast 8 a.m. Dinner 12.45 p.m. Tea 5 p.m. Supper 9 p.m. No servant to take any knives or forks nor on any account to remove provisions nor ale or beer out of the Hall.
>
> No gambling of any description nor oaths nor abusive language are on any account to be allowed.
>
> No servant is to receive any Visitor, Friend or Relative

* Cakes, preserves, drinks, ices etc. were made in the stillroom

14 *A housekeeper and other domestic servants (1886)*

into the house except by a written order from the House-keeper.

The Hall door is to be finally closed at half past ten o'clock every night after which time no person will be admitted into the house except those on special leave.

The rich saw the servants who worked for them at meal-times. At other times servants were supposed to keep out of sight. Their place was 'below stairs', in the basement. The biggest houses had special back stairs and corridors for them. When Lady Diana Cooper was a child she stayed at Belvoir Castle. Much later she described some of the servants.

There were the lamp and candle men, at least three of them. They polished and scraped the wax off the candelabra, cut wicks, poured paraffin oil and unblackened glass chimneys. After dark they were busy turning wicks up or down,

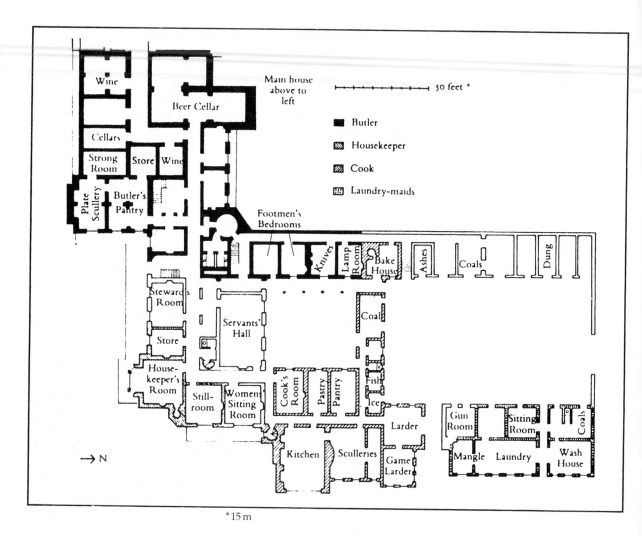

Main house
above to
left

⊢———+———+———+———+———⊣ 50 feet *

■ Butler

▨ Housekeeper

▧ Cook

▦ Laundry-maids

Wine

Beer Cellar

Cellars

Strong
Room

Store Wine

Plate
Scullery

Butler's
Pantry

Footmen's
Bedrooms

Knives

Lamp
Room

Bake
House

Ashes

Coals

Dung

Steward's
Room

Servants'
Hall

Coal

Store

House-
keeper's
Room

Still-
room

Women's
Sitting
Room

Cook's
Room

Pastry
Pantry

Fish

Ice

Gun
Room

Sitting
Room

Coals

→ N

Larder

Kitchen

Sculleries

Game
Larder

Mangle

Laundry

Wash
House

*15 m

15 *'Below stairs' at Lynford Hall, Norfolk*

snuffing candles. The watermen were the biggest people I had ever seen. They wore brown clothes, no collar and thick green baize aprons. On their shoulders they carried a wooden yoke from which hung two gigantic cans of water. Above the ground floor there was not a drop of hot water so their job was to keep all jugs, cans and kettles full in the bedrooms, and morning and evening to bring the hot water for the hip baths.

If anyone had the nerve to be abed until eleven o'clock there were many strange callers at the door. First the housemaid scouring the steel grate and encouraging the fire of the night before. Next the unearthly water giants. Then a muffled knock given by a knee, for the coal-man's hands were too dirty and too full. He was much like his brothers of the water but blacker far. He growled the single word 'Coal-man' and refilled one's bin.

The Rainbow Comes and Goes, 1958

1 How many servants worked at Holkham Hall?
2 What did a year's wages for all the servants add up to?
3 Copy the plan of the servants' floor at Lynford Hall. The maids' bedrooms were not on this floor; they were in the attic. Why?
4 Imagine you have just come to work at Holkham Hall. Write a letter home to tell your parents what clothes you wear (look at Picture 14), what rules you have to obey, and what you think about your clothes and the rules.

Becoming a servant

The huge numbers of servants who served the rich had nearly all started their career when still very young. Working families needed their children to earn money as soon as possible. It was hard for girls especially to find many other jobs to go to. Flora Thompson was brought up in a little Oxfordshire village. She later wrote about the life of the country people. She explained how girls became servants.

There was no girl over twelve or thirteen living permanently at home. Some were sent out to their first place at eleven. As soon as a little girl approached school-leaving age her mother would say, 'About time you was earnin' your own livin', me gal.' From that time onward the child was made to feel herself one too many in the overcrowded home. The girls, while at home, could earn nothing. Then there was the sleeping problem. None of the cottages had more than two bedrooms, and the departure of even one small girl of twelve made a little more room for those remaining.

Places were found for them locally in the households of tradesmen, schoolmasters, stud grooms or farm bailiffs. The first places were called 'petty' places and looked upon as stepping stones to better things. The employers were usually very kind to these small maids. The wages were small, often only a shilling a week. Caps and aprons and morning print dresses, if worn, were provided by the employer.

When the girls had been in their petty places a year their mothers began to say it was time they 'bettered themselves' and the clergyman's daughter was consulted. Did she know if a scullery-maid was required at any of the big country houses around? When the place was found the girl set out alone on what was usually her first train journey, with her yellow tin trunk tied up with thick cord, her bunch of flowers and brown paper parcel bursting with left-overs.

Lark Rise to Candleford, 1945

Flora went along with a local girl of twelve who was trying to find a job. They walked over the fields to a large house. The lady of the house took them into the kitchen. She spoke to Flora's friend.

'So you want a place?' she asked. Yes, she wanted a maid and she thought Martha might do. What could she do? Anything she was told? Could she get up at six without being called? There would be the kitchen range to light and the flues to be swept once a week and the dining room to be swept and dusted and the fire lighted before breakfast. After breakfast Martha would help her with the beds, turning over the rooms, paring the potatoes and so on; and after dinner there was plenty to do—washing up, cleaning knives and boots and polishing silver. And so she went on mapping out Martha's day until nine o'clock she would be free to go to bed after placing hot water in her mistress's bedroom.

Martha was bewildered. She stood, twisting her scarf, curtseying, and saying 'Yes, mum' to everything.

'Then, as wages, I can offer you two pounds ten [shillings] a year. It is not a great wage, but you are very small, and you'll have an easy place and a comfortable home.'

16 Seven o'clock in the morning

Martha's father would not let her take the job. He believed the house was haunted.

1 Martha's family may well have seen the job she went for advertised in the paper. Make up the advertisement that she answered. Mention the work and wages, but try to make the job sound attractive.
2 Look at Picture 16. Is the fireplace area the maid is cleaning different in any way from yours?
3 Look at Picture 17. What do you think the maid in the picture might have been saying to herself as she prepared to work?

Female servants

Families that could only afford one or two servants usually employed girls. They paid them lower wages than menservants. The housekeeper was in charge of the female servants.

Families with young children often paid for a governess. Since the governess had to teach the children she had to be well educated herself. Many governesses were the daughters of clergymen who did not have much money. Although Charlotte Brontë eventually became a famous writer, she was a governess for a while. Her father was the church minister at the lonely Yorkshire village of Haworth. Charlotte went to work for the Sidgwick family. She was very lonely and wrote to her sister Emily,

I have striven hard to be pleased with my new situation. The country, the house and the grounds are divine but, alack-a-day, there is such a thing as seeing all beautiful around you and not having a free moment or a free thought left to enjoy them. The children are constantly with me. As for correcting them I quickly found that was out of the question, they are to do as they like. A complaint to the mother only brings black looks on myself. I said in my last letter that Mrs Sidgwick does not know me. I begin to find she does not intend to know me, that she cares nothing about me except to contrive how the greatest possible quantity of labour may be got out of me and to that end she overwhelms me with oceans of needlework, muslin nightcaps to make and above all dolls to dress. I see more clearly than I have ever done before that a private governess has no existence, is not counted as a living rational being, except as connected with the wearisome duties she has to fulfil.

Mrs E. Gaskell, quoted in *Life of Charlotte Brontë*, 1857

A governess was often lonely. Her education made her different from other servants, yet she was not one of the family.

Life was also lonely for the girl who worked for a family who could only afford one servant. She had a great many duties to carry out yet no other servants to talk to. This is how an eighteen-year-old girl explained what her life as an only servant had been like when she first began work at the age of thirteen.

I didn't know nothing about anything. I didn't know where to buy the wood for the fire. I was frightened, oh I was. They wasn't particular kind on my first place. I had to do all the work. I'd no one to go to. Oh, I cried the first night. I used to cry so.

Then I got a place where there was nine children. I was about fourteen then. I earned two shillings a week. I used to get up and light the fire, bath them and dress them and get their breakfast. I'd take them all out for a walk on the common. Then there was dinner to wash up after and then by that time it would be tea time again. And then I had to put the children to bed and bath them and clean up the

19 *A kitchen in a country house (1850)*

rooms and the fires at night. And then there would be the gentleman's supper to get. I wasn't in bed till twelve and I'd be up by six.

The Cornhill Magazine, May 1874

In homes where there were many servants, some women worked in the kitchen, preparing and cooking food, washing up and cleaning. Others looked after the different rooms, cleaning out fires, sweeping the floors and dusting. Big houses usually had laundry rooms. Here servants boiled up water, washed, scrubbed, dried and ironed all day long. There were few modern machines to make work easy. A servant cleaned a floor by scattering damp sand or tea leaves (to gather the dust) then sweeping vigorously. Irons were solid lumps of metal that had to be heated on the fire. Servants spent a lot of time cleaning out coal fire grates, keeping the black iron around the fire smart, fetching coal and sweeping out soot. Flora Thompson described the lives of girls who became servants.

The girls who went into the kitchen began as scullery-maids, washing up stacks of dishes, cleaning saucepans and dish covers, preparing vegetables and doing the kitchen scrubbing and other rough work. After a year or two of this, they became under kitchen-maids and worked up until they were second in command to the cook. Some girls preferred house to kitchen work and they would be found a place as third or fourth housemaid and work upwards.

20 *Working a box mangle*

The maids on the lower rungs of the ladder seldom saw their employers. The upper servants were their real mistresses and they treated beginners as a sergeant treated recruits, drilling them well in their duties by dint of much scolding.

The food of the maids was wholesome and abundant, though far from dainty. In some houses they would be given cold beef or mutton or even hot Irish stew for breakfast. Their bedrooms were poor, but sleeping in a large attic shared with two or three others was not then looked upon as a hardship. The maids had no bathroom. A hip bath was part of the furniture of the maids' room. Like the children of the family they had no evenings out unless they had somewhere definite to go and obtained special leave. They had to go to church on Sunday.

Lark Rise to Candleford, 1945

1 Write a sentence about each of the following to explain their work: a kitchen-maid, a housemaid, a laundry-maid.
2 Look at Picture 19. How is the kitchen lit? What sort of materials are the containers made from? How do they differ from those of today?
3 Draw a picture of the box mangle (Picture 20). Next to it write a sentence to explain how it works.

Male servants

The servant in charge of other menservants was usually the steward. In some houses a butler held this position. In big country houses many men were needed to look after the gardens and the outside of the buildings. There were jobs inside for several men too. Very rich families paid a chef to run the kitchen, not a cook. The butler looked after the wines and was in charge of serving meals. Footmen helped serve meals, answered the door and carried messages. They usually wore very splendid, colourful uniforms and had to powder their hair. Only fairly tall men became footmen—their employers wanted them to look as impressive as possible. William Lanceley began work at sixteen. He went to join the staff of the local squire's home.

My wages were to be eight pounds a year with plenty of good food besides; clothes found except underclothing and boots. I was then told in a confidential manner that if I looked well after the visiting ladies' maids, cleaned their boots nicely and got the luggage up quickly I should pick up a nice little bit in tips, which proved correct.

Quoted in J. Burnett, *Useful Toil*, 1974

Although Victorian servants worked long hours and did not have much freedom, some of them lived very comfortably. They were fed, clothed and housed, which saved them a great deal of money. They were sure of work all the year round. Male servants probably did especially well. They usually only worked for families that were very wealthy. It was quite common for retired stewards and butlers to set up in business on their own, using money they had saved. The famous London hotel called Claridges was started by Mr and Mrs Claridge, a former butler and housekeeper.

The diary kept by William Taylor shows the advantages as well as the disadvantages of being a servant. He worked for a rich widow and was paid at least £40 a year. But when he married he still had to stay in his employer's home. His wife

21 *A butler cleaning the silver in his pantry*

22 *The kitchen at Minley Manor in the 1890s*

lived separately, nearby; William visited her on as many Sundays as possible. These are some of his actual diary entries.

Jan. 1st. I am the only manservant here. Here are three maidservants. I got up at half past seven, cleaned the boys' clothes [the boys were visitors] and knives and lamps, got the parlour breakfast, lit my pantry fire, cleared breakfast and washed it away, dressed myself, went to church, came back, got [served] parlour lunch, had my dinner, sit by the fire and red the Penny Magazine and opened the door when any visiters came. At four o'clock had my tea, took the lamps and candles up into the drawing room, shut the shutters, layed the cloth for dinner, took the dinner up, waited at dinner, brought the things down, washed up, had my supper at nine, took down the lamps and candles at half past ten and went to bed at eleven.

23 A footman and a maid

9th Jan. Up at eight. I am very fond of my Bed this cold weather. I spent this morning at work and fiddleing about the afternoon. I done a little drawing until between three and four when, to my great surprise, my Aunt Puzey called to see me.

12th Jan. I jenerally wait until ten o'clock [for breakfast] when my apatite has come and I can then get a cup of coco which I am very fond of and a rowl. This day we had for dinner a piece of surloin of beef, roasted brocoli and potatoes and preserved damson pie. We all have tea together at four o'clock with bread and butter and sometimes a cake. At nine o'clock we have supper: this evening its cold beef and damson pie. We keeps plenty of good table ale in the house and everyone can have as much as they like.

Dec. 30th. The life of a gentleman servant is something like that of a bird shut up in a cage. The bird is well housed and well fed but is deprived of liberty. In London most menservants has to sleep downstairs underground which is generally very damp.

Quoted in *Useful Toil*, 1974

1 From what you have read in this section make up an advertisement as if you were a rich person who needed a footman. Mention the hours, the pay, the work, the clothes, and the sort of person you are looking for.

2 Look at Picture 23. What do you think the maid might be thinking about the splendidly dressed footman who is carrying a letter on a silver dish?

3 Explain in your own words what you think William Taylor meant when he wrote that his life was 'like that of a bird shut up in a cage'. What special difficulties of his own might he have been thinking of?

4 From all you have read in this chapter what would you choose as the most important reason (a) for becoming a servant, (b) for not becoming a servant? Give a reason for your answers.

5 William Taylor was making a scrapbook. Imagine you are William and show what two pages of your scrapbook look like. The whole of this chapter will give you ideas. Include any stories, information or drawings that you found interesting.

3 Hard at Work

The ordinary people of Victorian Britain had to work very hard. Their hours of work were long, their free time was usually just one day a week. The money they earned was too little to give most of them a comfortable life and some of them were very badly off (see Chapter 5, 'The Poor'). Working life began as soon as a child could do something useful; it ended when illness or old age made working impossible. The people of nineteenth-century Britain could not expect to retire and live on old-age pensions. There were none to be had.

Children at work

During the early 1840s Parliament decided to investigate children's working conditions. The commissioners who carried out this work were horrified by what they discovered in Britain's industries and mines. They reported,

> Instances occur in which children begin to work as early as 3 or 4 years of age, not infrequently at 5, while in general regular employment commences between 7 and 8.
>   In many trades and manufactures children have not good and sufficient food, nor warm and decent clothing, great numbers of them when questioned stating that they have seldom or never enough to eat and many of them being clothed in rags.
> *Parliamentary Papers*, 1843, *vol.* 13

Coal mines Many small children worked in coal mines. Tiny boys and girls operated the ventilation systems; crouched in dark passages they opened and closed trap doors. Sarah Gooder, aged eight, explained,

> I'm a trapper in the Gawber pit. It does not tire me but I have to trap without a light and I'm scared. Sometimes I sing when I have a light, but not in the dark. I daren't sing then. I don't like being in the pit.
> *Parliamentary Papers*, 1842, *vol.* 16

By the time children were ten they were able to work as coal shifters. They carried the coal in baskets, or dragged it along in truckloads. Ellison Jack, an eleven-year-old Scottish girl, carried coal up ladders from the coal face to the main pit shaft. She said,

24 *A child hiring fair in Spitalfields, London (1850)*

I have been working below 3 years on my father's account: he takes me down at 2 in the morning and I come up at 1 and 2 next afternoon. I go to bed at 6 at night to be ready for work next morning. I have to bear [carry] my burden up four ladders before I get to the main road which leads to the pit bottom. My task is [to fill] 4 or 5 tubs. I fill 5 tubs in 20 journeys. I have had the strap when I did not do my bidding.

Parliamentary Papers, 1842, *vol.* 15

Work in coal mines was dangerous. Children lost their way and were injured in accidents. Parliament was sufficiently horrified by the commissioners' reports to bring in a new law in 1842. No children under ten and no females at all were to work underground.

Older boys continued to work in the pits. Tom Mann started his working life down a coal mine.

25 *The reformer Lord Shaftesbury visiting a coal mine in the 1840s*

> My work was to take away the coal or dirt. For this there were boxes. I had to draw the box along. A piece of stout material was fitted on the boy around the waist. To this there was a chain attached and the boy would hook the chain to the box and, crawling on all fours, drag the box along. There were only candles enough for one each and these could not be carried, the boy had to crawl dragging his load in darkness. Many a time did I lie down groaning.
>
> *Tom Mann's Memoirs*, 1923

Youngsters in the mines had to find their way around a maze of dark passageways. Sometimes they got lost. This happened to William Withers, though he was lucky enough to be rescued. Afterwards he remembered what happened.

> After I lost my light I found that I was lost and in a strange road. I could hear my Father at work all Friday. I knocked the side and made as much noise as I possibly could but no one answered me. They all went out that night leaving me there. I cried very much. I thought I saw the stars two or three times although I was a hundred yards underground. I saved my dinner as much as I could, only eating a bit at a time. The whole time I had been wandering about in the dark when I heard the hauliers and made my way to them.
>
> Quoted in J. R. Leifchild, *Our Coal and our Coal Pits,*
> *by a Traveller Underground*, 1853

Other work done by children Parliament's commissioners looked at other work done by children. They found that children worked in factories and workshops. Their hours of work were usually very long and they often spent their days in unhealthy surroundings. Jacob Ball, aged twelve, worked in a factory that made pottery.

I come in the morning to work at 6 o'clock, gets fires in, sweeps my place, get coals up and ash out. I go home to breakfast and sometimes takes my half hour. I go home to dinner at half past one. My hour allowed me is from 1 to 2 but John Wareham (the man in charge) won't allow me to go before. I always come back at 2 and go home sometimes at 8 or 9. I am very tired when I get home a-nights. Get my supper and go to bed and up again at half past five. If I were to cut away from work at 6 I should play me a bit. I should like to go to school, evenings; I should do that too.
Parliamentary Papers, 1843, *vol.* 14

The commissioners found that many children were harshly punished when they made mistakes. A boy of twelve who made nails said,

Some of the boys are not well treated by the masters, they don't get enough [food]. Knows a boy that makes scraps [bad nails] and somebody took him and put his head down on an iron counter and hammered a nail through one ear.
Parliamentary Papers, 1843, *vol.* 15

Girls carried out work that was just as hard and tiring as that done by boys. Sarah Griffiths, aged twelve, worked at making bricks. The commissioner who spoke to her reported that she

works from 6 in the morning till 8 or 9 at night. Is sometimes very tired at night; has to carry very heavy weights, bricks or clay, the girls sometimes fall down with them or drop them and spoil them, and have to bring them back; then they get smacked or turned off from work.
Finds her legs swell and has pains and aches between the shoulders.
Parliamentary Papers, 1843, *vol.* 15

From 1842 to 1867 Parliament made a number of laws that reduced the hours children worked in mines and factories. But even the famous Act of 1847, which limited the time women and children were to work to ten hours a day, allowed children to work 58 hours a week (five ten-hour days and eight hours on Saturdays). Many children worked in small workshops or at home. Here the new laws did not apply. In 1862 Mary Thorpe of Nottingham described how her sister made gloves at home.

My little sister, now five and a half years old, can stitch a good many little fingers and is very clever, having been at it for two years. She used to stand on a stool so as to be able to see up to the candle on the table. Little children are kept up shamefully late if there is work, especially on Thursday and Friday nights when it is often till eleven or twelve.

Parliamentary Papers, 1862, *vol.* 10

Small children did some jobs better than adults. One of the hardest of these was climbing up the many long twisting chimneys of large houses and sweeping down the soot made by coal fires. A Nottingham sweep, George Ruff, explained how sweeps toughened up boys for their work.

The flesh must be hardened. This is done by rubbing it, chiefly on the elbows and knees, with the strongest brine [salt water]. You must stand over them with a cane or coax them by a promise or a halfpenny if they will stand a few more rubs. At first they will come back from their work with their arms and knees streaming with blood and the knees looking as if the caps had been pulled off. Then they must be rubbed with brine again and perhaps go off at once to another chimney.

The best age for teaching boys is about six. But I have known at least two of my neighbours' children begin at the age of five. Seven or eight years ago a boy was smothered in a chimney here. The doctor who opened his body said that they had pulled his heart and liver all over the place in dragging him down.

Parliamentary Papers, 1863, *vol.* 18

A law of 1875 finally stopped sweeps using climbing boys.

Many children earned a little money by wandering city streets and selling things. This little girl told a journalist,

I go about the streets with water cresses crying 'Four bunches a penny! Water cresses!' I am just eight years old. On and off I've been near a twelve month on the streets. I used to help my mother who was in the fur trade and if there were any slits in the fur I'd sew them up. My mother learned me to needlework and to knit when I was about five. I bears the cold—you must—so I puts my hands under my shawl.

Sometimes I make a great deal of money. One day I took one shilling and sixpence and the cresses cost sixpence. But it isn't often I get such luck as that. I oftener makes threepence or fourpence. I don't have no dinner. Mother gives me two slices of bread and butter and a cup of tea for breakfast and then I go till tea and has the same. I've got some toys at home. I've a fireplace, a knife and fork and two little chairs. I never had no doll.

Quoted in H. Mayhew,
London Labour and the London Poor, 1851

By the 1880s children had to go to school until they were twelve or thirteen. Yet many went on working once their school day was over, as an Edinburgh boy explained.

If you didn't work, you didn't eat. It was a very common sight to see in Edinburgh children going about in the snow with no boots on. I used to work a fair amount after school hours, sometimes till eleven at night, the shops never shut till eleven at night. It was very hard work, messenger boy really; we had no bicycles to ride on. We used to carry the stuff on our head. I think for the whole week's job I got five shillings working about sixty hours.

Sergeant Major Anderson quoted in T. Barker (ed.),
The Long March of Everyman, 1975

Children left school to go straight into a life of hard work. Robert Sherard saw a little girl of fourteen busy in an iron works. He wrote,

I never saw such little arms and her hands were made to cradle dolls. She was making links for chain harrows and as she worked she sang. I saw her owner approach with a clenched fist and heard him say 'I'll give you "Some golden hair was hanging down her back". Why don't you get on with your work?' Next to her was a female wisp who was forging dog chains. She worked 10 hours a day.

The White Slaves of England, 1897

1 List three different jobs done by children in Victorian times.
2 Give two reasons why so many children worked at this time.
3 How many hours a day did Ellison Jack and Jacob Ball work?
4 Look at Picture 24. The children were keen to work. Write a newspaper story about the meeting. Mention how crowds of excited people gather, a policeman comes and then the employers arrive. The children try to attract the employers' attention. Some are picked for jobs.
5 What do you think William Withers' father said to him after his adventure?
6 Imagine you are a reformer of the 1840s who is speaking in Parliament to persuade MPs to pass a law to reduce the work done by children. Mention the hours children work and the harmful results of making them work, and suggest how you think children should be spending their time.

Adults at work

Many of the jobs that adults did were unhealthy and even dangerous. Nineteenth-century factories, homes and railways needed huge quantities of coal. But the coal was cut in a very primitive way. A writer who struggled along to a pit face saw this scene.

> In a small corner-like recess full of floating coal dust, foul air and refuse, glimmer 3 or 4 candles stuck in clay. Close scrutiny will discover one hewer [miner] nearly naked, lying upon his back, elevating his small sharp pick-axe a little above his nose and picking into the coal seam with might and main.
>
> *The Cornhill Magazine*, 1862

Miners needed to be brave just to work their way to the pit face in some mines. An old miner called Dave Douglass said,

> The thin seams of Durham are a nightmare and many's the nightmare I've had about them since. Crawling down the seam only inches would separate the roof from your body. Crawling was called 'belly flopper'; you would 'swim' forward, arms straight out in front, wriggling forward, and always the roof, bumping and creaking inches above your head.
>
> Quoted in R. Samuel (ed.),
> *Miners, Quarrymen and Salt Workers*, 1977

Many men worked in iron foundries and engineering workshops. Robert Sherard, a clergyman's son who became a

26 Pitmen hewing coal (1871)

journalist, visited an iron works.

> The heat of the furnaces is terrible and the work most exhausting. The men have to wring their clothes when they go home. The work is unhealthy and dangerous. Disease carries the men off [kills them] at an early age. 'The work affects you all over,' said a worker to me, 'You gets so cold that you shivers so you can't hold your food. The furnaces burn your insides out of you.' This man had burns all over his body.
>
> *The White Slaves of England*, 1897

Some men had jobs that did not keep them busy all the year. Henry Mayhew talked to a dock worker who told him,

> I am the foreman. I work under a publican who contracts with the ship owner to do the work of unloading the vessel. At this time of year [winter] each man is paid 3/6 [3 shillings and 6 pence] for his day's work. It is seldom that my gang of men has a full week's work, they are not employed above 3 days in the week. For 3 months there will be hardly anything doing in the timber ships. During this slack time the men have to go off to any job.
>
> H. Mayhew, *The Morning Chronicle*, 1849–50

John Ward was a cotton weaver in a Lancashire mill. He kept a

27 The ironworks at Poplar, east London (1863)

diary from 1860 to 1864. The diary shows how even factory workers could not depend on regular wages.

> April 10th, 1864. The mill I work in was stopped all last winter. When we started work again we can earn very little. I have not earned a shilling a day this last month and there are many like me. My clothes and bedding is wearing out very fast and I have no means of getting any more as what wages I get does hardly keep me.
>
> *Diary of John Ward of Clitheroe*

Women's hours were just as long as those worked by men. Textile mill owners liked to employ women. They paid them lower wages than they paid men doing similar tasks. A visitor to Glasgow went to a cotton mill.

> The place was full of women, young, all of them, some large with child and obliged to stand 12 hours each day. Their hours are from 5 in the morning to 7 in the evening, 2 hours of that being for rest. The heat was excessive, the stink pestiferous. The young women were all pale, thin, all with bare feet.
>
> R. E. Leader, *Life and Letters of J. A. Roebuck*, 1897

Textile workers did not have to carry out very heavy work. But some women did jobs that were very tiring.

28 *Cotton workers (1851)*

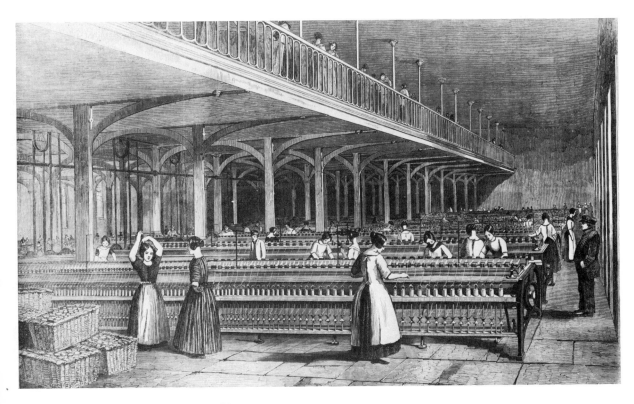

A writer who worked for a magazine called *The Edinburgh Review* visited a coal mine in the English Midlands and afterwards wrote,

> Of the groups engaged above ground the most remarkable are composed of the young women who work on the pit mounds; they take charge of the baskets of coal. They load the coal in trucks. They separate the ironstone from the shale. This is heavy and dirty work and the pit girls who are engaged in it with their shabby dresses tied about them and their bonnets stuck on the top of their heads seem not less sordid, but have an air of robust health.
>
> *The Edinburgh Review*, April 1863

30 *Women brickmakers at work*

Women laboured at other heavy and dirty jobs, like making bricks. A journalist who visited a brickworks reported,

> I found the girls at work making bricks in a low shed having no windows or openings for light except for the doorway. They temper it with their bare feet, moving rapidly about the clay, water reaching to the calf of the leg. This completed they grasp with both arms a lump of clay weighing about thirty-five pounds and supporting it upon their bosoms they carry this load to the moulding table where other girls mould it into bricks. They have to feed and attend to the furnaces used for heating the floors.
>
> *The Morning Chronicle*, 1886

Many men and women spent most of their lives working in small workshops. Here they might make clothes, or buttons, or metal objects such as nails or chains. Robert Sherard wrote about the work of a woman who made chains in a workshop at Cradley Heath in the Midlands.

> Work consisted of making heavy chains at 5/4 a hundredweight. By working for about twelve hours a day she could make one and a half hundredweight a week. Her hands were badly blistered and she was burnt in different parts of the body by flying sparks. I came across sheds with 5 or 6 women each working on her anvil. They are all talking

above the din of their hammers and the clanking of their chains or they may be singing: the misery is only too visible, be it in the foul rags and boots that the women wear, or in their haggard faces and the faces of the wizened infants hanging on their mothers' breasts as these ply the hammer.

The work of chainmaking consists in heating the iron rods, bending the red-hot piece, cutting in, twisting the link, inserting it into the last link of the chain, and welding on, closing it with repeated blows.

The White Slaves of England, 1897

At this time a family of five needed well over a pound a week to pay the rent and buy enough food.

1 Using Picture 26 and the descriptions of coal mining write a short newspaper article called 'My Day down the Pit'. Describe how you reach the coal face and the sights you see there.
2 Choose one of the figures shown in Picture 28. Draw the person and the tools nearby. Next to the drawing write a sentence explaining the work done by this person.
3 Use Picture 30 and the description of brick making to make up a story called 'My First Day at Work'.
4 About how much a week did Cradley chainmakers earn if they made 1½ hundredweights of chain?
5 Look at Picture 30 and read the extract about brickworkers. Now design an advertisement to bring workers to your brickworks. Mention the work to be done and the sort of clothes it would be best to wear.

On strike

Working people did not all quietly accept very long hours and low wages. Some began to organise trade unions. The first successful unions were for skilled and quite well-paid men like the Amalgamated Society of Engineers. There were a number of disputes between workers and their employers. One of the most famous took place in 1888 at Bryant and May's match factory. Mrs Annie Besant visited the factory to find out about the conditions in which women worked. She reported,

The hour for commencing work is 6.30 a.m. in summer and 8.00 in winter; work concludes at 6.0 p.m. Half an hour is allowed for breakfast and an hour for dinner. A typical case is that of a girl of 16, she earns four shillings a week and lives with a sister who earns as much as eight or nine shillings a week.

The splendid salary of four shillings is subject to fines. If the feet are dirty or the ground under the bench is left untidy, a fine of threepence is inflicted, for putting matches that have caught fire during the work on the bench one

32 *Matchworkers at Bryant and May's (1888)*

shilling has been forfeited. One department consists of taking matches out of a frame and putting them into boxes, about 3 frames can be done in an hour and a halfpenny is paid for each frame emptied. The girls have to run downstairs and upstairs each time to fetch a frame. One of the delights of the frame work is the accidental firing of the matches, when this happens the worker loses the work and if the frame is injured she is fined.

Quoted in E. Royston Pike,
Human Documents of the Age of the Forsytes, 1969

Many people read this article. The factory manager tried to get his workers to sign a paper saying they were well treated. When they refused he sacked a girl he thought was a leader. All 1,400 women in the factory went on strike. So many important people agreed that the match girls were badly treated that Bryant and

May gave in. Mrs Besant wrote,

> It was finally agreed that all fines should be abolished, deductions for paint, brushes, stamps etc. should be put an end to, all the girls should be taken back, the firm hoped the girls would form a union; they promised to see about providing a room for meals away from the work; they also promised to provide barrows for carrying the boxes which have been hitherto carried by young girls on their heads.

1 Imagine you work in the match factory. Write a letter to a newspaper to explain why you are on strike.

Struggling to manage

Working people had to get up early. Most did not have alarm clocks and paid a penny or two a week to a 'knocker up', who went round tapping on windows with a long pole. They dressed in clothes that were usually very dull in colour. Their clothes had to last many years and, when badly worn, were cut down and given to their children to wear. Working people kept warm by wearing as many layers of clothing as possible. When Lucy Luck set off for the silk mill she was quite well dressed. She said,

> I can never remember anything but cotton dresses, the old fashioned lilac-print capes like over-dresses in the summer and shawls in the winter, good strong petticoats and thick nailed boots both summer and winter, big coal-scuttle bonnets.

> Quoted in J. Burnett, *Useful Toil*, 1974

Lucy was fortunate to have boots. Many young people went barefoot in summer and sometimes in winter too. A German visitor to Manchester watched people hurrying to work in the cotton mills. He wrote,

> The clothing of the working people in the majority of cases is in a very bad condition. Wool and linen have almost vanished from the wardrobe and cotton has taken their place. Shirts are made of bleached or coloured cotton goods, the dresses of the women are chiefly of cotton print goods. The men wear trousers of heavy cotton and jackets or coats of the same. Hats are the universal head covering in England even for working men; round, high, broad-brimmed, narrow-brimmed, only the younger men wearing caps. Anyone who does not own a hat folds himself a low square paper cap.
> F. Engels, *The Condition of the Working Class in England*, 1845

Many of the pictures in this book give more detail of the sort of clothes working-class Victorians used to wear.

33 *A working-class home in London (1872)*

Working-class homes were usually overcrowded. Many families lived in just one or two rooms. But some better-paid people were able to afford a little comfort. Coal miners' cottages were described by a journalist.

> In nearly all the cottages the furniture is of a superior order. The bedstead is pretty sure to be a mahogany four-poster, it is placed in the best room as an ornamental piece of furniture and beside it will frequently stand a mahogany chest of drawers. An old fashioned 8 day clock usually flanks the four poster. In the best ordered pit dwellings I have often seen also good chairs, china, brass candlesticks and ornaments.

The Cornhill Magazine, 1860

Women who worked had a particularly hard time. The long working day meant they had little time and energy left for washing, cooking, cleaning and shopping.

This is how a man whose job it was to inspect working conditions in factories described the day of women who lived in the Stoke-on-Trent area. A woman had, he wrote,

> Half an hour to dress and suckle her infant and carry it out to nurse; one hour for household duties before leaving home; half an hour for actually travelling to the mill; 12 hours actual labour; one and a half hours for meals; half an hour for returning home at night; one and a half hours for household duties, leaving six and a half hours for recreation and sleep.
>
> Quoted in J. Calder, *The Victorian Home*, 1977

Many families found that they could only manage by borrowing money from a pawnshop. They left the shopkeeper one of their possessions that was worth a little money. They got it back

34 A pawnbroker's shop

when payday came. This is what one pawnshop was like.

> The shop had two entrances, one leading to the sales counter which was open and the other to the pledge counter which was divided off by partitions so that shy customers could not see one another. At one end of the pledge counter was a desk where one of the assistants made out a pawn ticket, one for the client and the other for an apprentice to pin to the pledge.
>
> Saturday night and Monday morning were of course the busiest time. On Mondays the women brought in their family's Sunday best—the husband's suit, boots, and often his watch and chain, the girls' frocks, dresses, shoes and shawls. Temporarily embarrassed housewives would come in with all kinds of other things—clocks, ornaments and pieces of furniture, sheets, rings, carpets and blankets, even wedding rings and flat irons.
>
> *The Times*, 19 October 1961

Victorian people faced not only long days of work, but an endless struggle to manage once they returned home.

1 Imagine you are opening up a pawnshop. Design a big poster to put up outside your new shop. Mention how helpful you intend to be, the sort of things you are prepared to take, and how the customers will be able to trust you with their secrets.
2 The 'knocker-up' had to get up very early. As he went round waking people he would see some folk setting off early for work. He would find some people hard to wake. Some might not be pleased to be woken. Write a short story called 'A Knocker-up's Morning' in which you mention as many of these things as possible.
3 Read the description of the colliers' cottages. Imagine you are the son or daughter of a miner who has just moved into a cottage like these with his wife and family. Write a page in your diary in which you say how pleased you are with your new home and all its contents.

4   The Poor

Exploring the unknown

Imagine you are standing, late one night, in a dark London street. It is 8 January in the year 1866. A horse-drawn carriage rumbles down the street, then

> The door of the carriage opened into the dark and muddy road. From that door emerged a sly and ruffianly figure marked with every sign of squalor. He was dressed in what had once been a snuff-brown coat, too small, and only made to meet across his chest by a bit of twine. The man's hands were plunged into his pockets and he shuffled hastily along in boots which were the boots of a tramp.
>
> J. Greenwood, *A Night in a Workhouse*, 1866

The author of this description and the tramp were the same man—James Greenwood. He was a writer, not at all poor, but determined to try to find out what it was like to be really poor. Other rich Victorians explored the poorest parts of Britain, too. What they discovered horrified them. One of the most famous of them was Seebohm Rowntree, the son of a very successful chocolate manufacturer. He explored his home town, York, and found that

> in this land of abounding wealth probably more than one fourth of the population are living in poverty. No civilisation can be sound which has at its base this mass of stunted human life.
>
> B. S. Rowntree, *Poverty, A Study of Town Life*, 1901

1 List all the things Greenwood had done to make himself look like a poor man.
2 Not all the tricks of disguise he used are mentioned here. Try to think of other things he would have to do if he was not going to be found out.
3 Imagine Greenwood returning to his comfortable home next day having seen children like those shown in Picture 35. Write a conversation he might have had with one of his family in which he tries to describe the appearance of the children.

The poor

Rowntree and others like him tried to find out why there were so many very poor people. Rowntree wrote,

> The wages paid for unskilled labour in York are insufficient to provide food, shelter, clothing adequate to maintain a

35 Poor children in London (an engraving by Gustav Doré)

family of moderate size in a state of bare physical efficiency. The life of a labourer is marked by several periods. During early childhood he will probably be in poverty, this will last till he begins to earn some money to add to the father's wage. If he has saved enough this 'prosperity' may continue after marriage until he has two or three children when poverty will overtake him. When the children are earning he enjoys another period of prosperity only to sink back into poverty when he is too old to work.

Poverty, A Study of Town Life, 1901

William Booth, the man who founded the Salvation Army, interviewed people like this man found wandering by the Thames in London. The man told him,

I've slept here two nights. I'm a confectioner by trade. I come from Dartford. I got turned off because I'm getting elderly. They can get young men cheaper and I have the rheumatism so bad. I've earned nothing these two days. I thought I could get a job at Woolwich so I walked there but could get nothing. I found a bit of bread in the road wrapped in a bit of newspaper. That did me yesterday. I'm 54 years old.

Darkest England and the Way Out, 1890

36 Sleeping out in London

1 From what you have read in this section, give some reasons why people lived in poverty.
2 Is 54 too old for work today? Why might Victorian workmen be worn out sooner than workers today?
3 Imagine you are the woman in Picture 36. You are being interviewed by William Booth. Tell him how you came to be there.

The slums

Friedrich Engels was a German who had a successful business in England. He spent much of his time writing about the poor.

> Every great town has one or more slums. True, poverty often dwells in hidden alleys, close to the palaces of the rich, but in general a separate territory has been given it where, removed from the sight of the happier classes, it may struggle along.
>
> *The Condition of the Working Classes in England*, 1845

Another foreign visitor was the French writer, Hippolyte Taine. In 1862, he explored slums in Liverpool.

> In the neighbourhood of Leeds Street there are 15 or 20 streets with ropes stretched across them where rags and underwear were hung out to dry. Every stairway swarms with children, the eldest nursing the baby; their faces are pale, the rags they wear are full of holes, they have neither shoes nor stockings and they are vilely dirty.
>
> *Notes on England*, quoted in *The Daily News*, 1872

George Sims, a wealthy Londoner, went to see one slum home in 1882.

37 The homes of the poor

We walk along a narrow dirty passage into a square full of refuse. The windows above and below are broken. To the door comes a poor woman, white and thin and sickly looking. She carries a girl; behind her, clutching at her scanty dress are 2 or 3 other children. We ask to see the room. What a room! The walls are damp and crumbling, the ceiling is black and peeling off, the floor is rotten and broken away in places and the wind and rain sweep in through gaps that seem everywhere. The woman, her husband and her 6 children live, eat and sleep in this one room and for this they pay 3/- a week.

How the Poor Live, 1883

1 Why would poor homes be crowded close together near where the poor worked?
2 Find and list all the signs of poverty mentioned in the last two extracts.
3 What sort of illnesses might result from living like this?
4 Look at Picture 37. Where do people obtain water? Why is there a channel in the street? Write a description of the street.

5 Look through all the information you have gathered. Then imagine you have just returned from visiting a slum and *either* write a newspaper article to try to shock the rich into caring about the problem *or* design a cartoon or poster that will have the same effect.

Inside the slum home In 1851 Henry Mayhew, a Londoner who spent a lot of time interviewing the poor for his newspaper, *The Morning Chronicle*, visited a fruitseller's home. Inside,

> A few sacks were thrown over an old palliasse [a mattress filled with straw], a blanket seemed to be used for a quilt, there were no fire irons or fender, no cooking utensils. Beside the bed was an old chest serving for a chair while a board resting on a trestle did duty for a table.
>
> Quoted in E. Gauldie, *Cruel Habitations*, 1974

Homes were lit with candles, or oil or paraffin lamps. Poorer people only began to have gas lighting after the invention in 1890 of the slot meter.

Not all poor people had quite so little as the fruitseller. But all poor people found it a struggle to be able to afford enough good food. In 1864 Dr Edward Smith travelled around Britain, collecting facts about what ordinary people could afford to eat. He wrote,

> In very poor families the children are fed at breakfast and supper chiefly upon bread, bread and treacle or bread and butter with tea, whilst at dinner they have the same food with boiled potatoes or cabbage smeared over with a little fat from the bacon with which it was boiled. On Sundays they usually have a better dinner.
>
> Quoted in J. Burnett, *Plenty and Want*, 1979

38 *A cotton worker's home in Manchester (1862)*

By 1897 Robert Sherard, a journalist, found that in the Midlands area where he lived, even people with jobs found it difficult to feed their families. He spoke to a woman whose job was making chains and wrote later,

> This woman had 6 children to keep and her husband, for he had been out of work since Christmas. Most often she had to beg dripping as a relish to the insufficient bread. The children had been weaned on 'sop', a preparation of bread and hot water flavoured with the drippings of the teapot. In good weeks she could get a bit of margarine and each week she bought a quarter of tea and four pounds of sugar. For clothes she depends on charity.
>
> *The White Slaves of England*, 1897

In 1883 Andrew Mearns worked for a group of churches as their secretary. What he saw of life inside slum houses filled him with horror and he wrote down many details of the life lived by the poor, such as these:

> Here is a mother who has taken away whatever articles of clothing she can strip from her four little children without leaving them naked. She has pawned them for coal and food.
>
> A poor woman reduced almost to a skeleton lives in a single room with a drunken husband and five children. She was eating a few green peas. The children were gone to gather some sticks wherewith a fire might be made to boil four potatoes.
>
> At the top of a house lives a family. The mother was nursing a baby 6 weeks old that had never had anything but one old rag around it. There were six children, barefooted; the few rags on them scarcely clothed their nakedness.
>
> *The Bitter Cry of Outcast London*, 1883

1 List the items of food mentioned in the extracts. What foods that you often eat are not on the list? How would the kind of food poor people ate have affected their health?
2 Read the extract describing the fruitseller's home then try to draw a picture of the scene as you imagine it was.
3 Food, clothing, lighting and furniture have all been mentioned. Imagine you are a rich person visiting a poor family at a mealtime and write a description of your visit, mentioning all these things.
4 What signs of poverty are there in Picture 38?

Official help

Government ministers and local officials tried to do something about the slums. In 1875 a law was passed giving councils power to pull down slum houses. In Birmingham the Lord Mayor,

Joseph Chamberlain, ordered the worst slums to be pulled down. A clergyman, the Reverend Dale, described how the councillors felt.

> They spoke of sweeping away streets in which it was not possible to live a healthy and clean life and of making the town cleaner, sweeter, brighter.
>
> Quoted in K. Dawson and P. Wall,
> *Public Health and Housing*, 1970

But Andrew Mearns did not think this new law was a change for the better.

> The Artisans' Dwelling Act has, in some respects, made matters worse. Large spaces have been cleared of fever-breeding rookeries to make way for the building of decent habitations, but the rents of these are far beyond the means of the poor. They are driven to crowd more closely together in the few stifling places left to them.

A few local councils did start to build homes to be rented to ordinary people, but not until the end of the century after local councils had been given extra powers.

Poor people could also get help with their bills if they could prove that they were deserving cases. The people they had to persuade were the Poor Law Guardians (in Scotland the Parochial Boards). The money came from local rates. This is what happened at one February meeting of a Parochial Board in 1863 in a part of north-east Scotland called Kennethmont.

> Application from J.D. for some assistance. The Board agree to allow her some oatmeal.
> Application from F.L. for a pair of blankets. Granted.
> Application from Mrs S. for a pair of shoes. Granted.
> The Inspector reported that as J.B. could not keep his daughter any longer he had arranged with Widow Howie to keep her at seven shillings a week.

1 Why did the Artisans' Dwelling Act make life worse for the poor?
2 Imagine you are one of the officials in Picture 39 who has listened to the applicant's pleas for help and seen her faint from hunger. What would you say to the other Guardians? What action would you suggest?

Workhouses

At the beginning of this chapter James Greenwood had disguised himself as a tramp. He described later how he entered a dark building and went into

> a space about 30 feet by 30 feet, on 3 sides a dingy white-washed wall roofed with naked tiles furred with damp and filth. The 4th side was boarded in for a third of its breadth,

54

39 *Jenny before the Board of Guardians. She is a poor person who has come to seek help from the Guardians and has fainted*

the remaining space being hung with flimsy canvas. This shed was paved with stone, the flags thickly encrusted with filth. Men lay over the flagstones on narrow bags scantily stuffed with hay, provided with a rug. Touzled, dirty, villainous, they squatted up in their beds and smoked foul pipes, 2 or 3 wore no shirts at all, their bodies fully exposed in the light of the single flaring jet of gas fixed high upon the wall.

A Night in a Workhouse, 1866

This room was part of a building known as a workhouse. They were to be found throughout Britain. Greenwood had entered a section of Lambeth Workhouse called 'the casual ward'. Here he found people with nowhere to live but well enough to work.

1 How is the room in Picture 40 lit?
2 How are the people trying to keep warm?
3 Write a list of the different clothes shown here. What adjectives would you use to describe these clothes?
4 List all the words and phrases in Greenwood's description that show the workhouse was an unhealthy place.

40 A men's 'casual ward' in a west London workhouse (about 1860)

Men in workhouse casual wards did not stay for long, but other men, women and children spent years of their lives in the workhouses. People who could not look after themselves went to workhouses only when they were absolutely desperate. Workhouse life was deliberately made harsh so that no one would choose to go there rather than work. In 1892 George Lansbury, who came from a very poor home but had risen to become a Councillor in Poplar, in east London, visited the local workhouse. After his visit he wrote,

> It was easy for me to understand why the poor dreaded and hated these places; all these prison sort of surroundings were organised for the purpose of making decent people endure any suffering rather than enter. The sick and aged, lunatics and babies and children, able-bodied and tramps, all herded together in one huge range of buildings.
>
> Quoted in R. Postgate, *A Life of George Lansbury*, 1951

Many of the people in the workhouses were children. Most of these children were orphans or had been abandoned by their parents. John Rowlands, for example, was taken to the workhouse (at the age of six) by one of the family who were being paid to look after him. He did not know where he was going.

> At last Dick set me down from his shoulders before an immense stone building and passing through tall iron gates he pulled at a bell which I could hear clanging noisily in the distant interior. A sombre-faced stranger appeared at the door, seized me by the hand and drew me within. The door closed and I experienced the awful feeling of utter desolateness.
>
> Quoted in N. Longmate, *The Workhouse*, 1974

Children in workhouses were often harshly treated. In 1858 a schoolteacher decribed a workhouse child.

> One day I saw a little girl with red eyes at our school (for they had no schoolmistress at the workhouse) whose heart seemed bursting and on enquiring the cause she said 'Missus has roped me'. Her back and arms were red and covered with great weals [sores] and marks of rope. The child told me that it was done for the merest trifle and that all the children told how it was the 'Missus's' habit to beat them with a thick hair rope. It had two knots at the end.
>
> Quoted in *The Workhouse*, 1974

They lived crowded together in rooms like the ones at Poplar that George Lansbury described in 1892.

> The buildings were built on the barrack system—that is long dormitories for scores of children to sleep in with very little accommodation for recreation. The children were dressed in the old hideous poor law garb, corduroy and hard blue serge and the girls with their hair almost shaved off.
>
> *A Life of George Lansbury*, 1951

Many elderly people also lived in workhouses. Because they were too old to find work they could not afford to stay in their own homes. A writer in 1872 saw that elderly couples who arrived at the workhouse door often suffered an unhappy fate.

> Couples who have been married as many as forty years are, for the last years of their lives, practically separated from one another. In a workhouse I know well, containing over a thousand aged inmates, there was only accommodation for twelve couples.

Most elderly couples were separated.

> Once a week they may meet for an hour to enjoy each other's society and perhaps fortify one another for next week's banishment.
>
> Quoted in *The Workhouse*, 1974

The people who ran the workhouses tried to feed the poor people in them as cheaply as possible. The Master at Andover ran his workhouse so cruelly that there was an investigation. It was found that

> some of the inmates in the workhouse were in the habit of eating raw potatoes and refuse food thrown to hogs and

fowls. Instances occurred in which inmates employed in
bone crushing ate the gristle and marrow of the bones they
were set to break.
Report of the Select Committee on the Andover Workhouse, 1846

Andover was an unusually cruel place. Most workhouse food
was like the meals described by James Reynolds, a shoemaker
who had been sent to Newmarket Workhouse when his business failed. In 1856 he wrote to his sister,

We've skilly for breakfast, at night bread and cheese,
And we eat it and then go to bed if you please.
Two days in the week we have pudding for dinner
And two we have broth, so like water, but thinner.
Two, meat and potatoes, of this none to spare,
One day bread and cheese, and this is our fare.
Quoted in *The Workhouse*, 1974

The poor were set to work. They broke stones for roadmaking,
turned handles to work flour mills, crushed bones to make
fertiliser. Many women worked at picking oakum. Mrs Mary
Higgs, a well-to-do lady who, like James Greenwood, disguised
herself as a tramp, described it.

Three of us were set to pick oakum. Do you know what
oakum is? A number of old ropes, some of them tarred,
some knotted, are cut into lengths; you have to twist and
unravel them inch by inch. After two hours I had, perhaps,
done a quarter of a pound and my fingers were getting sore,
while the pile before me seemed to diminish little.
The Tramp Ward, 1904

Workhouses were generally solidly built and clean. By the end of the nineteenth century they were not quite so harsh. Some of them had special sections where sick paupers were treated; elderly people were allowed a little tea and sugar; Bolton workhouse children even went on trips to Blackpool and to flower shows. But poor people still feared and hated the workhouses.

1   From all the information in this section, list the different sorts of people to be found in a workhouse.
2   Using the verse, make up a menu for a week's meals in a workhouse.
3   Imagine you are the little girl in the foreground of Picture 42. You have just come into the workhouse. Write a conversation you have with another girl who has been there many months. She will tell you about the clothes you have to wear, the food you have to eat, and the other people in the workhouse.

42 A workhouse yard

5 Living in the Country

When Victoria became Queen most British people lived in the countryside. Some owned their own farms but most worked for rich landlords.

These landlords had a lot of power over the people who lived on their lands. Some people thought they had too much power. In 1893 one of the people living on the Earl of Pembroke's lands grumbled,

> The labourer who wants to work in the parish must obtain employment on the Earl of Pembroke's land under one of the Earl's 2 farmers who will house him in one of the Earl's cottages, deducting the rent from his weekly wages. He sends his children to the national school (managed by the Earl's farmers) and goes to the church where he sits under

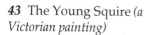

43 The Young Squire (*a Victorian painting*)

the eyes of the 2 churchwardens (Lord Pembroke's farmers again). When reduced to hopeless poverty he must apply for Poor Law relief to the 2 farmers. If the parish were a slave estate the condition of the inhabitants could hardly be more completely one of slavery.

Quoted in G. Avery, *Victorian People in Life and in Literature*, 1970

1 Make a list of all the ways in which a landlord controlled the lives of the people on his lands. Set it out as a newspaper article written by someone who does not like landlords. Begin 'Know the Truth! Did you know a landlord can . . .'.

At home

Farmworkers often lived in houses like these:

Thatched, built of cracked and ancient stud work [timber and plaster], containing one bedroom, one sitting room and one lean-to scullery. The bedroom in the roof, which was stopped with rags to keep out the rain, was approached by a steep ladder.

H. Rider Haggard, *Rural England*, 1906

In many places the land round the houses was in a filthy state. In a Dorset village, there was

a row of several labourers' cottages fronting the street in the middle of which is an open gutter. Behind the houses are placed the pigsties and privies. The matter [filth] constantly seeping from the pigsties and privies is allowed to find its way between the cottages into the gutter so that the cottages are nearly surrounded by streams of filth.

Quoted in P. Horn, *Labouring Life in the Victorian Countryside*, 1976

Inside, the furniture was rough and simple. In a Somerset cottage in 1872 there was

an old table and perhaps a broken chair. Seldom a vestige [small piece] of carpet on the floors. A few bedclothes, perhaps, huddled down in one corner. At night these had to be distributed among the several members of the family who, lying about on different parts of the floor, could not possibly in cold weather get a reasonable amount of warmth.

F. G. Heath, *The English Peasantry*, 1874

The people who lived in cottages like these could not afford to buy expensive food. Here is a verse written in Victorian times about a farmworker's food.

44 *A cottage in Warwickshire (1889)*

> He used to trample off to his work, while townsfolk were
> abed
> with nothing in his belly but a slice or two of bread.
> He dined upon potatoes, and he never dreamed of meat
> except a lump of bacon fat sometimes by way of treat.
> Quoted in J. Burnett, Plenty and Want, 1979

An old labourer explained what he and his family ate.

> For months at a time he had existed upon nothing but a diet
> of bread and onions, washed down when he was lucky
> with a little small beer. They had no tea but his wife imitated
> the appearance by soaking a burnt crust of bread in boiling
> water. I asked if his children, of whom there were eight,
> had lived on onions also. He answered no, they had
> generally a little cheese and butter.
> Rural England, 1906

A Yorkshire farmworker described his family's food.

45 A door-to-door tradesman (about 1900)

For tea there would be a basin of boiled milk with bread and bacon. Cups and saucers were never used, instead they had wooden basins for milk, mugs for tea and wooden trenchers at dinner for meat.

Quoted in *Labouring Life in the Victorian Countryside*, 1976

A girl born in Essex towards the end of the nineteenth century could remember her father grew much of their food in the cottage garden. But some things had to be bought.

Mother used to send us round to Mr Cooper the Butcher for a shilling's worth of pig's fry about once a week. This lasted our family of 9 for several days. Our diet consisted chiefly of a basin of porridge for tea, dripping toast for breakfast, plus a midday meal. We only had butter once a week on Sunday. My Mother used to bake her own bread and we children had to fetch the flour from the mill. A man came round with a basket of fish most Saturdays. We could also buy a small packet of tea for twopence, stewing steak, pork, sausages, and wild rabbits.

Essex Record Office, quoted in *Labouring Life in the Victorian Countryside*, 1976

Washdays were hard work for farmworkers' wives. They heated water in iron pots over the fire then tipped the water into large tubs. It was difficult to dry clothes quickly. Some families used mangles to squeeze water out of the clothes. A Norfolk girl who used the mangle at the local inn described it.

The mangle consisted of a huge box of large stones collected from the beach and it was worked with a large handle which, fastened to a large roller, propelled the box of stones back and forth. A charge of twopence was paid to the owner.

Norfolk Women's Institute, *Within Living Memory*, 1971

1 Look at Picture 44. What sort of materials have been used to build the cottage? What clues in the picture tell you it was an old building and not a modern one?
2 From what you have read in this section write out menus for the meals a farmworker would have eaten on an ordinary day.
3 Why do you think the labourer's wife tried to make a drink that looked like tea?

Work on a farm

Work on the farm began early in life. Children were expected to carry out all sorts of jobs.

They stop cattle straying, are sent to help scare birds, to

glean, to gather potatoes, to pop beans into holes at dibbling time, to pick hops, to gather apples, mushrooms and blackberries, to herd flocks of geese or turkeys, drive sheep to market, shred turnips, bring wood for the fire. They are mighty useful animals and as they get bigger they learn to drive a plough.

W. Howitt, *The Rural Life of England*, 1838

Many jobs were done by groups of children together.

Eight appears to be the ordinary age at which children join the gang, though seven is not unusual. One little girl only four years old was carried by her father to the fields and put to work. When the gangs are working at a considerable distance from home the children leave as early as five in the morning and do not return before eight at night. A little boy of only six years is stated to have regularly walked more than six miles out to work and often to come home so tired that he could scarcely stand. In winter the children often return from the fields crying from cold.

The Quarterly Review, 1867

A law was passed in 1867 stopping children under eight working in gangs.

By the time they were thirteen or fourteen boys were ready to start full-time work. Richard Hillyer was sent to a farm in Northamptonshire.

Every night I dropped asleep over my supper and then woke up just enough to crawl upstairs and fall into bed. Sunday was the only break. 'This is what it's going to be from now on,' I thought, 'lifting, hauling, shoving, trudging about from day to day.' It was like settling down into a deep bed of mud—cold, gluey.

Country Boy, 1966

Richard Hillyer was lucky. The local rector helped him to study and he escaped from farm life to Durham University.

The working day on the farm was a long one. In 1892 Richard Jefferies, who was the author of a number of books on farming, wrote,

> The ordinary adult farm labourer commonly rises at from 4 to 5 o'clock, if he is a milker and has to walk a little distance to his work, as early as half past three. At six he goes to breakfast which consists of a hunk of bread and cheese, now and then a piece of bacon. The time of leaving off work varies from half past five to half past six—in haymaking or harvest time often till eight.
>
> *The Toilers of the Field*, 1892

47 *A shepherd, his boy and his dog*

These long hours were filled with hard work. A young Yorkshireman, Fred Kitchen, grumbled,

> I waded through slop and cow-muck until I became absolutely lost. My breeches became so caked in pigswill, calf porridge and meal I believe they could have stood upright without me inside them.
>
> Artists have drawn pictures of the shepherd on the grassy uplands, but we have no picture of the shepherd in the muddy turnip field, sliding about in the muddy sheep pen, bending to clean out troughs or when snow and sleet swirls round their ears.
>
> *Brother to the Ox*, 1963

48 *A reaper at work (1890s)*

For all his work the farm labourer earned about ten shillings a week. By 1900 this wage had risen to around fifteen shillings. Women were paid less. This is the sort of work done by many young women in Cumberland and Northumberland.

> She takes up potatoes, she hoes turnips, she cleans the land of weeds and stones, she harrows at times, she leads the team [of horses] and drives the cart, she spreads muck and loads the dung cart, she cleans out the byre, and the pigsty, she makes hay, binds corn, and reaps with the sickle.
>
> Quoted in *Labouring Life in the Victorian Countryside*, 1976

Farmworkers frequently changed jobs. They searched for better wages and conditions by going to one of the 'hiring fairs' held twice a year in most country towns. Farmers inspected the men who gathered to look for work. Afterwards the countryside was alive with sights like this:

You cannot go far along country roads just now without meeting waggons piled up with the goods and chattels of farm hands changing quarters. They have been to some hiring fair and have got fresh places and here they are jogging about the country with their tables and chairs and beds and boxes and wives and children heaped up on the new master's waggon.

G. F. Millin, *Life in Our Villages by the Special Correspondent on The Daily News*, 1891

1 Imagine you are a 10-year-old country child visiting relatives who live in a town. Explain to them the work you do, your hours of work and how you feel by evening.
2 Why do you think children were expected to work so hard?
3 Look at the pictures which show farmworkers. Design an advertisement to be put up in the window of a shop selling clothes. List clothes suitable for farmworkers and, if possible, include drawings.

49 A hiring fair

Spare time

Farmworkers liked to gather in the village public house. The pub was plainly furnished. As you entered you had to

beware you do not knock your head against the smoke-blackened beams of the low ceiling and do not put your elbow carelessly on the table, stained with spilled ale, left uncleaned from last night, together with little heaps of

50 *The chimney corner in a Victorian public house*

ashes tipped from pipes and spots of grease from the tallow candles.

R. Jefferies, *Hodge and his Masters*, 1880

The other important building found in villages was the church. In Victorian times most places had not only a Church of England, but also a non-conformist Chapel.

On Sundays you will find in the church, if not the squire at any rate his household, the ladies of it almost certainly and the servants. Most of the large tenants come too, with their dependants. The gamekeeper's stalwart figure fills a seat. And with these must be numbered a sprinkling of the poor. In the chapel gather smaller tenants, artisans and shop-keepers with a sprinkling of free labourers and farm servants.

P. A. Graham, *The Rural Exodus: the Problem of the Village and the Town*, 1892

There were other activities too. Some villages had cricket teams, some boasted brass bands. Occasionally a travelling show toured the countryside. George Sanger described the show he and his fellow performers put on in the East Anglian village of Long Sutton.

We presented a lively programme of juggling, rope-walking, trick-riding. The last item was my fortune-telling pony. The last item was to tell the pony to find the biggest rogue. The proper response was to walk up to the ringmaster but on this occasion I saw the pony with his head resting on the shoulder of the village constable.

Seventy Years a Showman, 1966

By 1900 life in the Victorian countryside was changing. Some farmworkers got better cottages, and their pay improved. More machines were used on the land. But life in the countryside was still filled with very long hours of hard work; pay was still lower than in the towns and cities.

51 A threshing machine

1 What clue in this section tells you how many public houses were lit?

6 Good Health?

The Victorians were far more likely to be very ill than people in Britain today. Serious illnesses included typhoid, typhus, scarlet fever, smallpox, measles, diphtheria, tuberculosis and cholera. It was cholera that people feared most. It killed half of those who caught it. In 1848–9 cholera killed 15,000 of London's population. A person with cholera suffered terribly: he or she went blue in the face, had attacks of cramp, diarrhoea and vomiting. This is how one family suffered from cholera in 1866.

> On the evening of the 23rd September Mr G. had been seized with diarrhoea, sickness and cramps. His wife began to complain of discomfort and this developed to cholera. On the 30th September one of her daughters aged eight was seized with cholera and in a few hours died. That same night a serving lad in the house was seized with cholera and barely escaped with his life. On the 2nd October the doctor who was attending them died of cholera. On the 3rd October another daughter passed into cholera but recovered. On the 5th the maidservant got diarrhoea, fell into secondary fever with which she eventually died. On the 5th also a labourer who worked on the premises was taken with diarrhoea which passing to cholera, killed him. Mr G. got a very acute new attack and died. The grandmother eventually died on the 14th.
>
> *Privy Council Medical Reports*, 1866

People were not all equally at risk. Edwin Chadwick, an important reformer who tried to improve health in Britain, wrote down these figures in 1842.

Average age of death in:	Manchester	Rutlandshire
Professional persons and gentry and their families	38	52
Tradesmen, farmers and their families	20	41
Labourers and their families	17	38

1 What were the first signs of cholera?
2 Looking at the table, who do you think had the best chance of escaping serious illness?

The causes of illness

Dirt Many people lived in very unhealthy houses. For much of the nineteenth century thousands of homes did not have proper drains or sewers. Many houses in Leeds were

> wholly unprovided with any form of drainage or arrangements for cleansing, one mass of damp and filth. The ashes, garbage and filth of all kinds are thrown from the doors and windows of the houses upon the surface of the streets. The privies are few in proportion to the number of inhabitants. They are open to view both in front and rear and are invariably in a filthy condition and often remain without the removal of any portion of the filth for 6 months.
>
> *Parliamentary Papers*, 1845, *vol.* 3

Human waste piled up in holes in the ground. 'Nightmen' carried out the job of cleaning out these cesspits. In Manchester, a local inhabitant wrote,

52 Cholera spread quickly in the crowded and filthy slums

A COURT FOR KING CHOLERA.

53 London nightmen

The nightmen are very filthy in their appearance and habits and being often assisted in their labours by their families, their houses are usually most offensive and wretched abodes.

Parliamentary Papers, 1845, *vol.* 18

The nightmen tipped what they had gathered onto huge dung-heaps, often placed close to houses. In Greenock, Scotland, a local doctor reported,

In one part of Market Street is a dunghill, yet it is too large to be called a dunghill. I do not mistake its size when I say it contains 100 cubic yards of impure filth collected from all parts of the town. It is never removed; it is the stock in trade of a person who deals in dung; he retails [sells] it in cartfuls.

Parliamentary Papers, 1842, *vol.* 26

The dung was used to fertilise local farmland.

Foul water   In many towns the water people used for drinking and for cooking was filthy. The writer Charles Kingsley was very shocked by what he saw in part of London in 1849.

54 Poor people collecting water in east London

> I was yesterday over the cholera districts of Bermondsey and Oh God! What I saw! People having no water to drink, hundreds of them, but the water of the common sewer which stagnates, full of dead fish, cats and dogs.
>
> F. E. Kingsley (ed.), *Charles Kingsley: his Letters and Memories of his Life*, 1879

People collected their drinking water from streams and rivers into which sewers drained. Some drew water from taps or pumps and wells, queuing up to wait their turn. In 1840 in Liverpool,

> The water is turned on a certain number of hours during the day, four hours perhaps, each poor person fetches as much as they have pans to receive, but they are frequently not well supplied with these articles and in consequence are frequently out of water.
>
> *Parliamentary Papers*, 1840, *vol.* 11

55 *A slum tenement in Dundee*

Poor living conditions Diseases spread speedily through the overcrowded rooms of working-class homes. In 1883 Andrew Mearns was horrified by the London homes he visited.

> Every room in these rotten and reeking tenements houses a family, often two. In one cellar a sanitary inspector reports finding a father, mother, three children and four pigs. In another room a missionary found a man ill with smallpox, his wife just recovering from her eighth confinement, and the children running about half-naked and covered with dirt. Another apartment contains father, mother, and six children.
>
> *The Bitter Cry of Outcast London*, 1883

Food soon became infected. Cholera and typhoid spread in drinking water that contained sewage. Typhus, too, spread in dirty living conditions: it was passed from one person to another by lice. Tuberculosis was carried in infected milk.

Occasionally a cry of despair from the poor broke through to trouble the better-off. On 5 July 1849 *The Times* published this oddly spelled letter. It had 54 names scrawled beneath it.

> Sur,
>
> May be beg and beseech your proteckshion and power. We are Sur, as it may be, livin in a wilderness so far as the rest of London knows anything of us, or as the rich and great people care about. We live in muck and filthe. We aint got no privez, no dust bins, no water suplies, no drain or suer in the whole place. The Suer Company in Greek Street, Soho Square, all great and powerful men, take no notice wat somedever of our complaints. The stenche of a Gully hole is disgustin. We al of us suffer and numbers are ill and if the Colera comes Lord help us.

1 From all that you have read so far, make out a list of all the reasons why disease was common in Victorian times.
2 How do you think the 'nightmen' got their name?
3 Imagine you are the person who has put in the water supply shown in Picture 54. What sort of rules would you want local people to follow? Using the picture make up a notice to be nailed up by the tap.

Reforms

Even rich people sometimes caught serious illnesses. Members of Parliament could not fail to notice the foul state of the River Thames as it flowed past their meeting place. Dozens of sewers emptied their contents into the river.

In 1858 the smell from the Thames was so bad that people could not bear to stand near the river. It became known as the

DIPHTHERIA. SCROFULA. CHOLERA.

FATHER THAMES INTRODUCING HIS OFFSPRING TO THE FAIR CITY OF LONDON.

(A Design for a Fresco in the New Houses of Parliament.)

56 This cartoon from Punch *represents the River Thames as the father of the diseases that spread in London*

'Year of the Great Stink'. But at last the government began to pass laws to improve health. In 1871 it set up the Local Government Board to try to improve living conditions. In 1888 Parliament established county councils and county boroughs. These stronger and better organised local authorities tackled some of the unhealthy conditions in their areas. They provided proper sewers in pipes under the streets. Their engineers laid on supplies of pure water. The engineer in charge at one of the first places to do this (Nottingham) reported,

> At Nottingham the increase of personal cleanliness was at first very marked indeed, it was obvious in the streets. Before the supply was laid on in the houses water was sold chiefly to the labouring classes by carriers at the rate of ¼d a bucket.
>
> *Parliamentary Papers*, 1844, *vol.* 18

In London, Dr John Snow studied the way cholera seemed to be linked to water supplies. He concentrated on a particular pump in Broad Street, Soho. In 1855 he wrote,

> The result of the inquiry was that there had been no particular outbreak or increase of cholera in this particular part of London except among the persons who were in the habit of drinking the water of the above mentioned pump well.
> *On the Mode of the Communication of Cholera*, 1855

Doctors began to understand how disease spread. They persuaded local authorities to carry out changes. Henry Mayhew spoke to a workman in charge of a new water-pumping system of cleaning out cesspools. The workman said,

> I was one of the first set as worked a pump. There was a great many spectators. I dare say as there was forty scientific gentlemen. I've been on the sewers flushing and pumping ever since. The houses we clean out all say it's far the best plan, ours is. 'Never no more nightmen,' they say. You see our plan's far less trouble to the people in the house and there's no smell. In time the nightmen'll disappear. In course they must, there's so many new dodges comes up.
> *London Labour and the London Poor*, 1851

By 1900 Britain possessed a huge network of sewers and many vast new water-supply schemes. Many towns now had parks and gardens where people could enjoy fresh air. Cholera had been checked, and typhus, typhoid and smallpox were less serious. The country buzzed with new officials checking, inspecting, reporting and advising.

57 George Peabody, an American, left money to pay for homes to be built for workers in London. This drawing (1866) shows some of the Peabody homes. There are no gardens, but the houses are well built. Only working people who had steady jobs could live in these homes, as they had to be able to pay the rent

58 *A Glasgow street-cleaner*

1 Look at Picture 58. Describe the street-cleaner and say what kind of rubbish you think he is carrying in his basket.

Treating yourself

When ordinary people became ill they did not usually visit a doctor, for they had to pay for his services. They preferred to try to treat themselves. All sorts of odd 'cures' were popular. Some people believed that sniffing the air near a gasworks cured whooping cough. Others ate live snails as a way of treating tuberculosis. Shopkeepers and market stalls sold mixtures that claimed to cure almost everything.

Many Victorians took the dangerous drug opium to ease pain. Working mothers sometimes gave opium to their babies to keep them quiet. It was mixed with treacle and known as 'Godfrey's Cordial'.

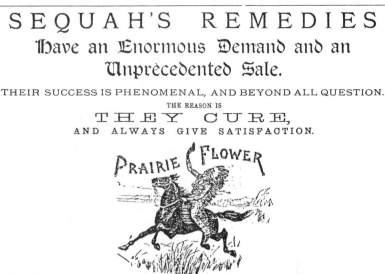

SEQUAH'S REMEDIES
Have an Enormous Demand and an Unprecedented Sale.

THEIR SUCCESS IS PHENOMENAL, AND BEYOND ALL QUESTION.

THE REASON IS

THEY CURE,
AND ALWAYS GIVE SATISFACTION.

PRAIRIE FLOWER

SEQUAH SPEAKS.

" With pride and pleasure I feel that I am doing much good to Mankind, as I am confident that by the use of these Remedies the following Diseases will succumb

Indigestion,	Heartburn,	Flatulence,
Biliousness,	Liver Complaint,	Constipation,
Loss of Appetite,	Headache,	Want of Ambition,
Pains in the Back,	Kidney Troubles,	Lumbago,
Sciatica,	Neuralgia,	Rheumatism,
	And Rheumatic Gout."	

These Peerless Remedies are prepared by the SEQUAH INDIAN MEDICINE FIRM, and are duly Registered and Protected.

Prairie Flower and Sequah's Oil

Are sold in Bottles, Price 2/-, by all Chemists and Dealers in Medicine.
SEE THAT THE NAME IS BLOWN IN EACH BOTTLE.

59 Newspapers often carried advertisements for pills and mixtures that claimed to cure many different illnesses

Mr Brown, the coroner of Nottingham, states that he knows Godfrey's Cordial is given on the day of birth! The druggist made up in one year, three hundredweight of treacle into Godfrey's Cordial—a preparation of opium exclusively consumed by infants. The result of this terrible practice is that a great number of infants perish, either suddenly from an overdose, or as more commonly happens, slowly, painfully...

Parliamentary Papers, 1843

Possibly the most famous of all pills produced in Victorian times were those made by Thomas Beecham. He advertised them as 'worth a guinea a box', but they were sold for just over a shilling. They actually cost an eighth of a penny to produce.

77

In 1896 three brothers produced and sold by post some tablets known as 'Lady Montrose's Miraculous Female Tabules'. The tablets claimed to help women who were expecting a child they did not want. The brothers kept the addresses of their 8,000 customers, and two years later sent them the following letter:

> Madame,
>
> I am in possession of letters of yours by which I can positively prove that you did commit the fearful crime of abortion by preventing or attempting to prevent yourself giving birth to a child. Either of these constitutes a criminal act punishable by penal servitude and legal proceedings have been commenced against you and your immediate arrest will be effected unless you send me on or before Tuesday morning the sum of £2. 2s. 0d being costs already incurred by me, and your solemn promise on oath before God that never again will you prevent or attempt to prevent yourself giving birth to a child.
>
> Charles J. Mitchell, Public Official.
>
> G. Perry and N. Mason, *Rule Britannia*, 1974

The brothers had collected £800 before the police caught them.

1 Imagine you are selling Godfrey's Cordial. Design a large poster to tell people how it can help them.
2 The advertisers liked to print letters from people who were supposed to be satisfied customers. Make up a letter that the makers of 'Sequah's Remedies' might have used to prove their goods could cure many different illnesses.

Hospital care

Some workhouses set up wards where sick people were treated. Until the 1880s these places were usually very unsatisfactory. In 1865 a visitor who went round several workhouses wrote,

> In a great and well ordered workhouse I visited the wards, in each were from 15 to 25 sick or helpless poor. In each ward all the assistance given and all the supervision were in the hands of a 'nurse' and a helper, both chosen from among the pauper women. The age of the nurses was from 65 to 80. I recollect seeing in a workhouse a ward in which were ten old women all helpless and bedridden; to nurse them a decrepit old woman of 70, lame and withered and feeble and her assistant was a girl with one eye. Only the other day I saw a pauper nurse in a sick ward who had a wooden leg!
>
> *The Workhouse Visiting Journal*, 1865, quoted in N. Longmate, *The Workhouse*, 1974

Some hospitals were set up with money left by rich people. But Florence Nightingale, who did so much to improve nursing, thought many were unsatisfactory, and wrote,

> The floors were made of ordinary wood, which owing to lack of cleaning and lack of sanitary convenience for the patients' use had become saturated with organic matter [human excreta] which when washed off gave off the smell of something quite other than soap and water. Walls and ceilings were also saturated with impurity. Heating was supplied by a single fire at the end of each ward. In some hospitals the windows were boarded up in winter. After a time the smell became sickening, walls streamed with moisture and vegetation appeared. The remedy for this was frequent lime washing but the workmen engaged on the task frequently became seriously ill.
>
> *Notes on Hospitals*, 1865

The nurses lived, cooked and slept in the wards. They had no proper training, their pay was poor and, as a result, many did not take their job seriously. Florence Nightingale had a low opinion of nursing in the 1850s.

> The nurses did not as a general rule wash patients, they never washed their feet and it was with difficulty and only in great haste that they could have a drop of water just to dab their hands and face. The beds on which the patients lay were dirty. It was common practice to put a new patient onto the same sheets used by the last occupant of the bed, and mattresses were generally of flock, sodden and seldom if ever cleaned.
>
> *Notes on Nursing*, 1860

People who needed operations before 1870 faced a risky experience. Doctors used brandy to drug their patients. They often did not bother about hygiene. They wore ordinary everyday clothes, operated on rough wooden tables and scattered sawdust on the floor to soak up the blood. Hospital care improved in the last 30 years of the nineteenth century. Poor people in workhouses were not allowed to work as nurses. Hospitals improved their training courses for doctors.

> At a great hospital like St Bartholomew's there was one operating day a week and the surgeons came into the theatre and operated in the oldest and dirtiest of frock coats they possessed. Surgery was something like a struggle in a shambles, the patient drugged with brandy having to be held down by half a dozen brawny assistants. It was the introduction of chloroform which altered this. Saved from

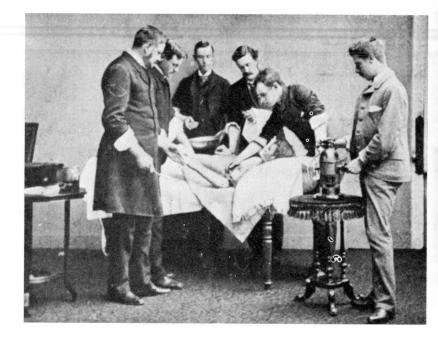

60 *An operation using a carbolic spray (1869)*

the cries and struggles of the patient, operations could be performed quietly. The advent of antiseptics and the teaching of Lister also suddenly increased enormously the possibilities of operating.

J. J. Abraham, *Harley Street and its Significance*, 1926

By 1900 a number of women had become doctors. This change only came about after a long struggle led by Elizabeth Garrett Anderson. When she tried to go to study at Middlesex Hospital the male students declared,

The presence of young females as spectators in the operating theatre is an outrage to our natural instincts and feelings and calculated to destroy these sentiments of respect and admiration with which the opposite sex is regarded by all right-minded men. The presence of a female student in the Middlesex School has become a byword and its members are subject to taunts.

J. Manton, *Elizabeth Garrett Anderson*, 1965

Elizabeth Garrett Anderson qualified by having private lessons and by going to foreign hospitals. Florence Nightingale greatly improved the career of nursing. Her parents tried to prevent her becoming a nurse. They thought it was not a suitable job for a well-brought up girl. She too went abroad to learn about proper health care. The terrible sufferings of British soldiers in the Crimean War (see Chapter 9) caused a great outcry in Britain. Florence Nightingale was asked to go out and improve the soldiers' hospital at Scutari. With a team of nurses she reorgan-

61 Florence Nightingale in the hospital at Scutari

ised it, cleaned it up and equipped it properly. One of the nurses who was with her wrote,

> Night is especially trying for the sick and wretched and then on all sides arose the moan of pain. At this period there were no night nurses, but Miss Nightingale, lamp in hand, each night traversed alone four miles of beds. How many lives this lady has been the means of saving during these rounds by calling medical aid is known only to herself. She was peculiarly skilled at the art of soothing, her gently sympathising voice and manner appeared always to refresh the sufferer.
>
> M. Goodman, *Experiences of an English Sister of Mercy*, 1862

After the war a grateful public raised £44,000 for Miss Nightingale. She used it to set up a nursing school.

Health care gradually improved in many ways. But much remained to be done. People had to pay more to visit a doctor than most of them could afford. There were not enough hospitals and many of them charged fees. Diphtheria and severe forms of measles, whooping cough and scarlet fever still raged. Tuberculosis was common. Millions of ill-fed people lived in dreadful homes. In 1896, of every 1,000 babies born alive, 163 had died before they were one year old.

1 List 3 things that you might not have liked if you had been a patient in one of the earlier Victorian hospitals.
2 List at least 3 ways in which medical care improved in the later years of Queen Victoria's reign.
3 Florence Nightingale's parents did not want her to become a nurse. Suggest some reasons why they did not think it was a suitable job for her.

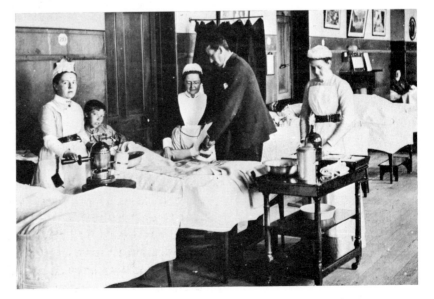

62 A ward in Aberdeen Infirmary in late Victorian times

7 At School

Many children living in Britain in the early nineteenth century did not go to school. Some rich people paid for their children to go to private schools; others hired tutors to teach their children at home. Ordinary children in Scotland had the best opportunity of going to school, for the Church of Scotland had set up schools throughout the country. But when parents needed children to work, they kept them away. In England some children learnt to read and write at Sunday schools. By 1900 this situation had completely changed. All children went to school until they were about thirteen years old.

Schools for the children of the rich

Early nineteenth-century boarding schools were very uncomfortable places. One of the most famous of these 'public' schools was Eton. A former pupil remembered his impressions of the great room where all the boys lived when he first saw it, at the age of ten.

> It was nearly dark and there were no lights except a few candles carried by the boys. The floor was covered with bedding, each bundle wrapped in a coarse horse rug. The noise and hooting of nearly 50 boys each trying to find his

63 *Eton College (1861)*

scanty stock of bedding combined with the shouts of the older boys calling their fags gave me a taste of my future. At 8 p.m. the doors were closed and we were left prisoners for the night.

I was appointed fag to a member of the VI Form. I had to count his linen, make lists for the laundress, fetch water for his basin from the outdoor pump. Breakfast consisted of a couple of rolls, some butter and a cup of milk. Fagging had become an organised system of cruelty. I was frequently kept up until one or two o'clock in the morning. I have been beaten on my palms with the back of a brush or struck on both sides of my face because I had not closed the shutter tight enough. I say nothing of having the tassel of one's nightcap set on fire in the night or having one's bed turned on end and finding one's heels in the air. The rioting and drinking that took place after the doors were closed can scarcely be credited. There was mutton for dinner daily. By the time the joint came to me there was little left but bone and my dinner generally consisted of excellent bread. Most of the bread was wasted as the elder boys used to pelt each other with it.

A. D. Coleridge, 'Eton in the Forties', quoted in C. Hollis, *Eton*, 1960

New headteachers gradually improved the public schools. Rugby School, under its famous Head Thomas Arnold, led the way in trying to give boys a better education. Thomas Hughes was a pupil there and afterwards wrote *Tom Brown's Schooldays*, a

64 *Rugby School (about 1870)*

65 *A Scottish day school*

story about life at Rugby. Tom Brown explained what a good public schoolboy should try to do:

> I want to be A1 at cricket and football and all the other games. I want to get into the Sixth and please the Doctor and I want to carry away just as much Latin and Greek as will take me through Oxford respectably and I want to leave behind me the name of a fellow who never bullied a little boy or turned his back on a big one.
>
> T. Hughes, *Tom Brown's Schooldays*, 1857

Boys were often sent away to school when about eight years old. Winston Churchill's parents decided their son should go to St George's School, Ascot. Winston Churchill explained what a shock this was to him.

> I was to go to school. I was now seven years old and I was what grown-up people in their off-hand way called 'a troublesome boy'. It appeared that I was to go away from home for many weeks at a stretch in order to do lessons under masters. The fateful day arrived. My mother took me to the station in a hansom cab. I was miserable at the idea of being left alone among all these strangers in this great fierce formidable place. After all I was only seven and I had been so happy in my nursery with all my toys.

He never settled down at school.

> Flogging with the birch was a great feature in its curriculum. Two or three times a month the whole school was marshalled in the library and one or more delinquents were hauled off to the adjoining apartment by the two head boys

and there flogged until they bled freely while the rest sat quaking, listening to their screams. How I hated this school.

My Early Life, 1930

Churchill's parents took him away from the school. A fellow pupil remembered him as a very naughty boy.

He had been flogged for taking sugar from the pantry and so far from being penitent [sorry] he had taken the Head-master's sacred straw hat from where it hung over the door and kicked it to pieces.

M. Baring, *The Puppet Show of Memory*, 1922

By 1900 most towns contained grammar schools. Well-to-do people paid to send their sons and daughters to these day schools.

Children in public schools and day schools spent much of their time studying English, Latin, Greek and Mathematics. History, Geography and French were becoming more popular but Science subjects were not studied by most pupils.

1 Explain in your own words what a 'fag' was.
2 Imagine you are writing home after your first dinner and night at Eton in the 1830s. Tell your parents about what you have seen and heard.

Different kinds of schools

Until 1870 Britain did not have a properly organised system of schools. There were several different types of school but even in 1870 only a third of children between ten and twelve went to any of them. Younger children were more likely to go to school, as they were not able to work a full day at many jobs. Yet a third of children under ten never went to school.

Some rich people believed the poor children roaming the streets often became criminals. They paid for schools to be set up to teach the poor honest ways. These 'ragged' schools were set up from the 1840s; their name came from the appearance of pupils like these Londoners:

When we first opened the School no less than five boys came absolutely naked except for their mother's shawls which were pinned around them. Five separate gangs of thieves attended the school, all of whom were, within six months, earning their livelihood more or less respectably.

C. Booth, *Life and Labour of the People in London* (17 vols), 1884–1903

The ragged schools tried to help children to become honest workers. But when Henry Mayhew went into the London

66 *London 'street arabs' being given food*

Drawn from Life 1886.

streets to gather information for his newspaper he heard a different point of view. A London policeman said,

> More reading and writing is a harm to a vicious child. It makes him steal more boldly and with more judgement for he sees the prices marked. The smartest thieves I've met with could all read and write.

A young thief agreed.

> At the ragged school I learned reading, writing, tailoring, shoemaking and cleaning the place. There were forty or fifty boys, half of them were thieves. We would teach any good boy to thieve.
>
> H. Mayhew, *London Labour and the London Poor*, 1851

Britain's workhouses contained thousands of children; they were all supposed to be given some sort of education. In the 1830s a Somerset clergyman visited Walcot workhouse school.

> We were conducted to a room in which about 30 little wretches stood in a class, a man holding a large whip standing in the midst. He was a pauper with only one eye. Seeing no books or slates we at first doubted whether this was the schoolroom and the following dialogue was the result.
> 'Are you the schoolmaster?'
> 'Yes.'
> 'What do you teach the children?'

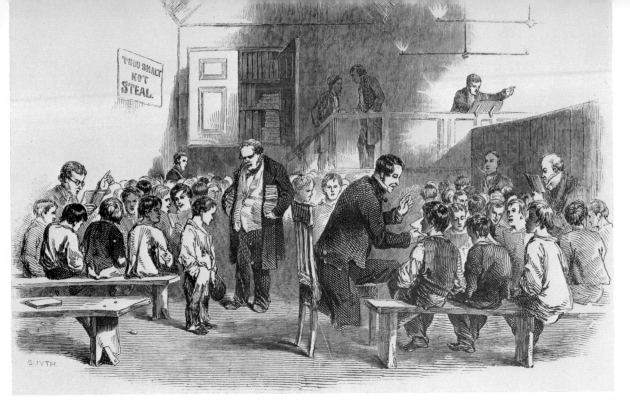

67 *Lambeth Ragged School in London (1846)*

'Nothing.'
'How then are they employed?'
'They do nothing.'
'What then do you do?'
'I keep them quiet.'
> R. A. Leach, *Pauper Children, their education and training,*
> *a complete handbook to the law*, 1890

Even as late as 1868 an inspector who visited workhouses found very low standards. In one school, he reported

> a total ignorance of the Bible and of arithmetic and blunders of every sort characterised their examination papers; the children apparently read fluently but on examining their books I found that many were held upside down. The children could not read at all but had been taught to repeat certain sentences and to hold their books before them as if they were reading.
> W. Chance, *Children under the Poor Law*, 1897

The ragged and workhouse schools were for special groups of children. Many children went to small privately-owned schools, often called 'dame' schools because they were run by elderly ladies. A pupil called John Sykes who went to one of these schools later remembered,

> My first school was an old woman's school, a very common village academy in those times with its rickety forms and its clean sanded stone floors, it was presided over by dames of

sixty or seventy years of age. When they could do nothing else they could keep a school.

Our fee was a penny per week. Our dame had her own way of controlling us by means of a leather lash tied to a stout walking stick. We frequently tried to get near the door and while the teacher dozed we manoeuvred to slip into the fields and lanes and into the sunshine.

Quoted in I. Stickland, *Voices of Children, 1700–1914*, 1973

Other children were educated in factory schools. Laws passed from 1833 limited the hours children worked in factories and made factory owners set up schools. The factory schools varied greatly. In Rochdale in 1861 an inspector found:

68 A group of children from a ragged school

> The private factory schools are on the whole unsatisfactory. In two, taught in cottage rooms by old incapacitated weavers, hardly any of the children learn writing and none could do more in reading than scramble through an easy verse in the New Testament.
>
> Quoted in P. Gosden, *How They Were Taught*, 1969

Yet in a factory in nearby Manchester the owners

> have provided a well warmed and well ventilated room, they have engaged a competent master and mistress. Reading, writing and arithmetic are taught to the children and the girls are taught needlework.
>
> Quoted in L. Evans and P. J. Pledger, *Contemporary Sources and Opinions in Modern British History*, 1967

1 Why do you think many workhouses and factories would not hire proper teachers?
2 Why did the policeman not approve of educating very poor children?
3 What clues in Picture 68 tell you these were poor children?
4 There is a notice on the wall of the drawing of Lambeth Ragged School (Picture 67). What other notices do you think the teachers might have put up? Design and draw one.

Church schools

The leaders of Britain's churches were very worried by the small number of schools that existed in the early nineteenth century. They feared that children would grow up unable to read the Bible and unable to earn an honest living. They began to set up schools and charged the pupils' parents a few pennies a week. In 1833 the government began providing a little money for these church schools. The politicians hoped that schooling would produce more capable workers and better behaved citizens. In 1841 a third of the men and nearly half the women who got married in England could not even write their names. When inspectors began visiting these Church schools in the 1830s they found many were like this one.

> The master and mistress, man and wife, are totally incompetent. The children are shamefully ignorant and the supply of books and apparatus is lamentably defective. No school at all would be better.
>
> *Report of the Committee of Council on Education*, 1850–51

Underpaid teachers struggled to teach huge classes of perhaps a hundred children of different ages. They used 'monitors' to help them, older children who passed on to pupils the lessons they learnt from the teacher. An inspector of 1845, describing

69 *A school run on the monitor system (1839). The toys are rewards for good work*

monitors, said that they were

> about eleven and a half years old, reading with ease but not much intelligence, writing from dictation without any regard to punctuation, working ordinary rules of arithmetic. The knowledge of geography, history or general information which the more intelligent of these youths may possess is not called for.
>
> *Report of the Committee of Council on Education*, 1845

Pupils learnt information written on the blackboard. Then they repeated what they had learnt like this.

> A Lesson on the Cup
> Monitor 'What is a cup made of?'
> Pupils   'Gold, silver, china.'
> Monitor 'Who drinks out of gold cups?'
> Pupils   'The king.'
> Monitor 'Who drinks out of china cups?'
> Pupils   'Poor people.'
> Monitor 'What is the inside of a cup?'
> Pupils   'Hollow.'
> Monitor 'The outside?'
> Pupils   'Convex.'
> Monitor 'What is the edge called?'
> Pupils   'The brim.'
>
> From a textbook of 1837

1 Imagine you are a teacher who is telling a new monitor exactly what he is to do.
2 What would a monitor's lesson on 'a plate' be like? Write out the questions and answers.

70 *A London School Board
'capture' in the middle of the night
(1871)*

Board schools

By 1870 the government had decided that it must improve Britain's schools. W. E. Forster was the person in charge of schools. He explained why changes were needed.

> We find a vast number of children badly taught or utterly untaught because there are too few schools and too many bad schools and because there are large numbers of parents who cannot or will not send their children to school.
>
> *Parliamentary Debates*, 1870

The government passed laws in 1870 (for England and Wales) and 1872 (for Scotland). It ordered every city, town and country area to choose a group of people to be called a 'School Board'. These School Boards set up new schools in their local areas. They paid for them with money from the rates and with money from the government. In ten years so many new Board Schools were opened that the government ordered parents to send children to school. There were now enough places to make this possible.

Most children stayed at school until they were thirteen, though some who passed a special 'labour certificate' examination left school a year earlier. Several thousand children did not go to school full-time. They spent half of every day at factory work. John Sykes was a full-time pupil who watched these 'half-timers' struggling in school.

The half-timers were the boys who worked in the mills morning and afternoon alternately. They often came to school with bleeding fingers. The lads were harshly treated at the mills. Bleeding heads and bleeding hands were often their portion and with this type of fingers they were expected to write. No wonder they sometimes fell asleep in the effort.

'Slawit in the Sixties', quoted in *Voices of Children*, 1973

The children crowded into their classrooms, sitting on hard wooden benches. Teachers often taught sixty or seventy pupils in one class. Walter Rose, a carpenter's son, went to one of these Board Schools. He wrote,

No one expected us to like school. Every morning at 9.0 o'clock we were rung into the schoolroom by a bell on the roof. We sang the morning hymn ('Awake My Soul') led by a harmonium which one of the monitors played. I do not remember ever singing another opening hymn. None of us knew the right wording.

A prayer by the master followed and then he mounted his platform desk and filled up the register while we were given a lesson from the Old Testament by a monitor. These readings were anything but dull to us; we took the side of the Israelites and revelled in the slaughter of wicked tribes. Now and then the monitor stopped and questioned us; those whose answers were wrong were called from their seats to stand in line at the front.

When the scripture lesson was over the master caned all the boys (and now and then a girl) who were standing out in line.

Good Neighbours, 1969

Most teachers were very strict. George Hewins was a pupil in a Stratford-on-Avon class. He watched his teacher punish two cheeky boys.

He tanned them and whaled their backs—we thought he were never going to stop. Whack! Whack! Whack! The skin was broke! We stared in silence, never said a word—we daren't.

Next morning we heard a cuffufle in the entrance. The

71 An Assembly at a Board School (1900)

two mothers had arrived. They said they'd smash him up. They'd have given him summat if they could have copped him, but he escaped out the back door.

Most of the time we was bored. Singing was the only thing you might say I enjoyed at school.

A. Hewins (ed.), *The Dillen*, 1981

The children in Board Schools learnt several subjects. In Flora Thompson's school,

Arithmetic was considered the most important of the subjects taught. The writing lesson consisted of the copying of copperplate maxims [sayings]: 'A fool and his money are soon parted', 'Waste not want not' and so on. Once a week composition would be set, usually in the form of writing a letter describing some recent event. History readers were in use containing such stories as Alfred and the cakes. No geography was taught. But on the walls of the classroom were hung splendid maps. Once a day a class would be called out for a reading lesson.

Her Majesty's Inspector of Schools came once a year.

F. Thompson, *Lark Rise to Candleford*, 1945

The Inspector tested what the children had learnt. He gave them sums to work out like this:

> Turn 5 years, 45 weeks, 5 days, 17 hours, 49 minutes into minutes. Write out your answer in words.
>
> *Good Neighbours*, 1969

He read out sentences which the children had to copy out correctly. The children wrote their answers on slates using special pencils that made a loud squeaking sound. He checked that the children had learnt parts of the Bible and sections of

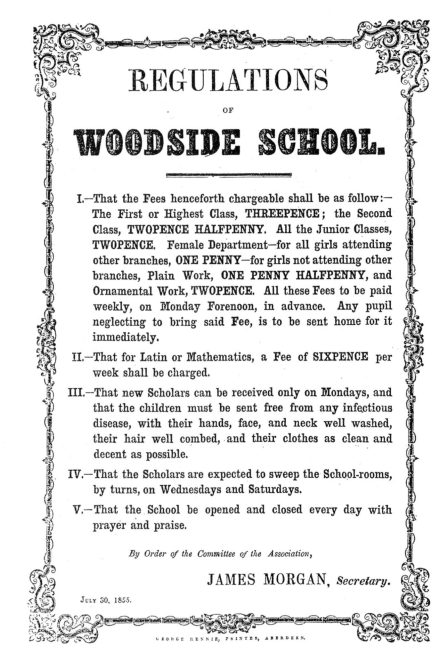

REGULATIONS

OF

WOODSIDE SCHOOL.

I.—That the Fees henceforth chargeable shall be as follow:— The First or Highest Class, **THREEPENCE**; the Second Class, **TWOPENCE HALFPENNY**. All the Junior Classes, **TWOPENCE**. Female Department—for all girls attending other branches, **ONE PENNY**—for girls not attending other branches, Plain Work, **ONE PENNY HALFPENNY**, and Ornamental Work, **TWOPENCE**. All these Fees to be paid weekly, on Monday Forenoon, in advance. Any pupil neglecting to bring said **Fee**, is to be sent home for it immediately.

II.—That for Latin or Mathematics, a Fee of **SIXPENCE** per week shall be charged.

III.—That new Scholars can be received only on Mondays, and that the children must be sent free from any infectious disease, with their hands, face, and neck well washed, their hair well combed, and their clothes as clean and decent as possible.

IV.—That the Scholars are expected to sweep the School-rooms, by turns, on Wednesdays and Saturdays.

V.—That the School be opened and closed every day with prayer and praise.

By Order of the Committee of the Association,

JAMES MORGAN, *Secretary.*

JULY 30, 1855.

GEORGE RENNIE, PRINTER, ABERDEEN.

72 Regulations for Woodside School, Aberdeen (1855)

history. Specially written books helped children prepare for these tests. This is part of one of them:

> Who was Henry VIII?
> The son of Henry VII.
> What was his character?
> As a young man he was bluff, generous, right royal and handsome.
> How was he when he grew older?
> He was bloated, vain, cruel and selfish.
>
> Dr Brewer, *My first book of the History of England*, 1864

At first children had to pay a few pennies a week to go to a Board School. If they wanted to learn more than Religion, Arithmetic, Reading and Writing they usually had to pay extra money. By 1900 these fees were abolished. A Board School teacher had to be able to teach many subjects. A young woman applying for a teaching post in 1879 wrote,

> I can teach Mathematics, French, Latin, Physical Geography, Domestic Economy (including Practical Cookery). I can give instruction in Freehand Drawing, Linear Perspective, Model Drawing, Landscape Drawing and Painting in water colours, in Needlecraft and Cutting Out, in Drill and in Vocal Music. I also understand the rudiments of German and Italian and possess a powerful Soprano Voice.
>
> M. C. Morris, *Yorkshire Reminiscences*, 1922

1 Imagine you are a 'half-time' pupil's parent. Write an 'excuse note' to the teacher to explain why your child has not been able to do school work properly.
2 Imagine you are a school inspector who has just visited and tested a class. Write a report to explain the different tests you gave and how well the children did.
3 Look at Picture 71. Write a list of all the clues in the picture that tell you it is not a modern classroom scene.
4 How does life in a Board School compare with life in your school today? List any things that seem to you to be the same, then list differences. Is the education provided in schools today better?

8 On the Move

During the nineteenth century the ways in which people travelled altered greatly. As early as 1850 a writer in *The Illustrated London News* saw important changes.

> Within the last two or three years people have been [able to] travel to distances which their forefathers had neither time nor money to undertake. The working class of thirty or even fifteen years ago did not know their own country. Very few travelled for pleasure beyond a small circle around the place which they inhabited.

Horse-drawn transport

Throughout the nineteenth century horse-drawn travel was important. When a Victorian family set off on a day's outing they were very likely to travel in a horse-drawn cart. Flora Thompson went on this sort of trip, riding in the local innkeeper's two-wheeled cart which her father had borrowed.

> Father and Mother rode in the front seat, the children were strapped into the high narrow seat with their backs to those of their parents, and off they went. From their high seat they could see over hedges into buttercup meadows where cows lay munching the wet grass and big cropping cart-horses loomed up out of the morning mist. 'Pat, pat, pat' went Polly's hooves in the dust, 'creak, creak, creak' went the harness, and 'rattle, rattle, rattle' went the iron-tyred wheels over the stony places. The farm carts and bakers' vans which passed that way on week-days were standing in yards with their shafts pointing skyward; the gentry's carriages reposed in lofty, stone-paved coach houses, and coachmen and carters and drivers were all still in bed, for it was Sunday.
>
> F. Thompson, *Lark Rise to Candleford*, 1945

Stagecoaches ran along Britain's main roads, carrying passengers on long journeys. They were not very comfortable. The Reverend Sydney Smith complained that the bumpy roads damaged both himself and his luggage.

> It took me nine hours to go from Taunton to Bath before the invention of railroads. In going from Taunton to Bath I suffered between 10,000 and 12,000 severe contusions [cuts and bruises]. As the basket of the stage coaches in which

73 *Ludgate Circus in London in 1872*

luggage was then carried had no springs, your clothes were rubbed all to pieces.

Quoted in C. W. Scott-Giles, *The Road Goes On*, 1946

After 1840 there were fewer and fewer stage coaches. They could not compete with the railways. In a verse written in 1840 a writer rejoiced that there would be

No drunken stage coachman to break people's necks
Turned o'er into ditches, sprawled out on your backs
No blustering guard that through some mistake
His blunderbuss fires if a mouse should but squeak.

R. Palmer, *A Touch on the Times*, 1974

74 *The Guildford coach (about 1895)*

The stage coaches stopped at inns so that both horses and travellers could rest. A writer in *The New Sporting Magazine* did not think much of the one he visited.

> Our travellers had been driven through the passage into a little dark dingy room at the back of the house with a rain be-spattered window, looking against a white-washed wall. The table which was covered with a thrice-used cloth was set out with lumps of bread, knives, and two and three pronged forks. Inside passengers viewed outside ones with suspicion. Presently the two dishes of pork, a couple of ducks and a lump of half-raw sadly mangled roast beef with waxy potatoes and overgrown cabbages were scattered along the table.

Many inns like this went out of business after 1850. In 1860 Henry Mayhew talked to a man who had worked in an inn.

> I was employed in a large coaching inn in Lancashire, but about ten years ago a railway line was opened and the coaching was no go any longer; it hadn't a chance to pay so the horses and all was sold and I was discharged with a lot of others.
>
> *London Labour and the London Poor*, 1851

Horse travel was chiefly used for short journeys in the later nineteenth century. Private carriages, hansom cabs (working as taxis) and horse-drawn buses trundled along the roads. Osbert Sitwell went in one of these buses and wrote later,

> The buses of those days had two large wheels in front and two smaller ones behind; they were painted red and white. Our vehicle was drawn by two fine horses and travelled at 8 mph. It carried about 14 persons on the top, which was

much lower than that of the motor bus today. The driver sat only just beneath with no shelter above his head.

The Scarlet Tree, 1946

1 Flora Thompson wrote about the 1880s. What sort of work were horses still being used for? Find as many examples as possible.
2 List all the different types of horse-drawn vehicles in Picture 73.
3 List at least three reasons why people were pleased not to have to use stage coaches any more.
4 Look at Picture 74. Imagine you are advertising the services of your stagecoach. Draw a picture of a coach; add writing that will persuade people to travel by coach.

Canals

Britain had a very large canal network. But barges sailed slowly, canals froze in winter, and in hilly areas canal-building was difficult. Thomas Boyle compared rail and canal travel in a book he wrote in 1848. He saw that trains were speedy and efficient. Powerful engines pulled the trucks and carriages.

The canal, on the contrary [represents] quiet plodding sluggishness. There is nothing fast about a canal. The miserable horse with his fodder-can eternally fixed to his mouth to save the trouble of feeding him at regular intervals, half-eating, half-sleeping, half-walking, half-pulling, proceeds listlessly on his journey. Delays are frequently made at the canal-side public houses.

T. Boyle, *Hope for the Canals!*, 1848

Many canals lost business to the railways after the 1830s.

75 A canal barge (1874)

1 Why did the coming of railways ruin many canals?
2 Look at Picture 75. What might the person in charge of the barge have said to explain why he still preferred barge-travel?

The coming of railways

When Victoria became queen there were few railway lines. By 1900 most towns and large villages had railway stations. Thousands of ordinary workmen carried out this amazing achievement of bringing railways to even remote parts of Britain. Thomas Roscoe watched these men cutting away a hillside.

> By day and night they struggled without relaxing and at night the hill literally swarmed with moving bodies lighted to their work by torches flickering from side to side and from place to place. Creaking cranes, dragging by ropes and pulleys the laden barrows in their guides and again slowly curbing their descent down the almost perpendicular banks, the clatter of continual footsteps, the heavy sound of spade and pickaxe and the busy hum of toiling men completed a scene of unexampled animation [activity].
> Quoted in C. Walker, *Thomas Brassey, Railway Builder*, 1969

The men who built the railways were called 'navvies'. They often worked in lonely areas, living in camps and wandering from job to job like this navvy.

> After I left home I started on the road, tramping about the country looking for work. Sometimes I'd stop a few weeks with one master and then go on again travelling about. I soon got into bad company and bad ways. Perhaps I'd light on an old mate somewhere and we'd go rambling together from one place to another. If we earned any money we'd go into a public house and stop there two or three days till we'd spent it all. We'd wander on till we could find a gang of men at work at some railroad. I went to work in Bradford where I stayed about 6 or 8 weeks. Here an engine was to start upon a new line and the contractor gave us a load of beer for the opening. Three of us got hold of a barrel, rolled it down the hill, knocked in the head of it and drank out of our hats.
> Quoted in J. Burnett, *Useful Toil*, 1974

The arrival of a large number of navvies often alarmed the local people. An engineer who helped to build the London–Birmingham line complained,

> These navvies are generally the terror of the surrounding country, they are as completely a class by themselves as the Gypsies. Possessed of all the daring recklessness of the

76 *Making a railway cutting in Camden, London (1836)*

smuggler, their ferocious behaviour can only be equalled by the brutality of their language. It may be truly said their hand is against every man, therefore every man's hand is against them and woe befall any women with the slightest shame or modesty whose ears they can assail. From being known to each other they in general act in concert [together] and put at defiance any local constabulary force; consequently crimes of the most atrocious character are common and robbery has been an everyday occurrence wherever they have been congregated in large numbers.

Quoted in T. Coleman, *The Navvies*, 1965

These men laid thousands of miles of track. They blasted rock, dug tunnels, and built bridges and embankments.

77 *A navvy camp that was more solidly built than many. The navvies clearly stayed here some time and were able to make gardens*

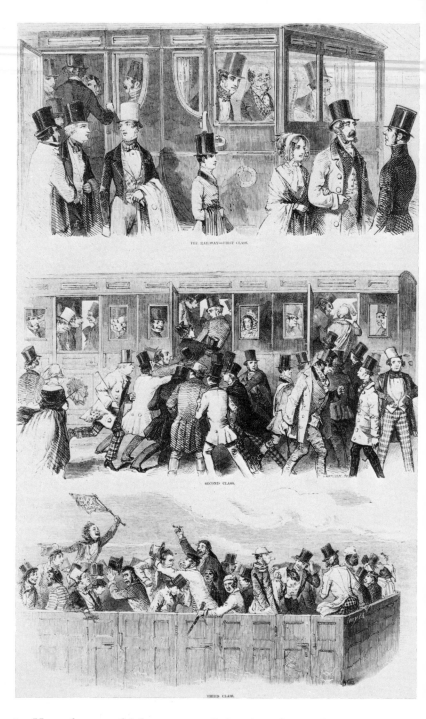

*78 Travelling by train—first,
second and third class (1847)*

1 How do you think someone living in a house by the Camden
   Cutting felt about the coming of the railway? Use Picture 76 to write
   a letter to a friend in the countryside. Describe all the sights and
   sounds.

2 How might a contractor get navvies to work for him? Design a bold
   simple poster to be put up in public houses to recruit navvies to a
   rail-building scheme.

Travelling by train   The first travellers by train felt a great sense of adventure. Those who could afford only the cheapest tickets had to ride in open waggons. It was very uncomfortable if it rained.

> If you turned your back on it it filled the nape of your neck, if you faced it you had overflowing pockets with an additional cataract from the front rim of your hat which before long was as limp as wet brown paper. Some people covered heads with handkerchiefs; it was only prolonging the misery as you did not know next where to put your handkerchief when you removed it. Everything was ruined from your health downwards.
>
>   A. R. Smith, *The Struggles and Adventures of Christopher Tadpole, at Home and Abroad*, 1848

There were books that advised travellers how to travel safely.

> Get as far from the engine as possible for three reasons. First, should an explosion take place you may happily get off with the loss of an arm or a leg. Secondly, the vibration is very much diminished the further you get from the engine. Thirdly, always sit with your back towards the engine, by this plan you will avoid being chilled by a cold current of air which passes through these open waggons, and also save you from being blinded by the small cinders which escape from the funnel.
>
>   F. Coghlan, *The Iron Road*, 1838

In 1844 the government ordered the railway companies to improve their services. They had to put roofs on the third-class carriages that ran on normal services. But open waggons were still sometimes used on special trains.

Early travellers had to take food with them or snatch a hasty bite when the train stopped at a station with a refreshment room.

Many early third-class carriages were not lit. In 1870 Francis Kilvert rode in one to Bath.

> The carriage was nearly full. In the Box Tunnel, as there was no lamp, the people began to strike foul brimstone matches and hand them to each other all down the carriage. The carriage was chock full of brimstone fumes, the windows both nearly shut, and by the time we got out of the tunnel I was almost suffocated. Then a gentleman tore a lady's pocket handkerchief in two, sized one fragment, blew his nose on it and put the rag in his pocket. She then seized his hat from his head.
>
>   W. Plomer (ed.), *Kilvert's Diary, 1870–79*, 1944

A · RAYLWAY · STATYON. SHOWYNGE Yᵉ TRAVELLERS · REFRESHYNGE · THEMSELVES.

79 *A cartoon showing passengers hurrying to get refreshments while the train stops at a station*

One traveller later recalled the problems caused by the lack of lavatories in many coaches.

> Fortunately after many hours the train stopped long enough at a small station in Northern England for the men to take to the woods and the females to make for the ladies' waiting room where a long queue formed outside the single WC. The maids—low in the pecking order as it were—had to use the coal scuttle.
>
> I. Smullen, *Taken for a Ride*, 1968

Travelling by train was sometimes dangerous. In 1863 *The Globe* complained,

> There is literally no security on any English railway against outrage, fire or murder. In a train going at full speed some women may be exposed to insult, two or more persons may be engaged in a struggle for life. The driver is bent on keeping time, the guard is beyond reach. The loudest screams are swallowed up by the roars of the rapidly revolving wheels and a murder may go on to the accompaniment of a train flying along.

In the 1890s railway companies began to put communication cords in carriages.

1 Look at Picture 78. How are the three sorts of carriage different? How do the clothes of travellers going by the different classes differ?

80 The station at Kyle of Lochalsh, Scotland

2 List at least three things that made early travel uncomfortable.
3 Look at Picture 79. How can you tell the train is ready to leave?
4 Write your own account of a Victorian train journey. Include a number of the ideas you have just read about (including a stop for refreshments) so that your journey is quite an eventful one. Write your account as if you work for a newspaper. You are trying to entertain your readers. Give your story a bold heading.

Changes brought by the railways The railways altered Britain's towns and cities. Rich people began to move to houses built well away from town centres. They travelled in to work or for shopping or entertainment by one of the speedy train services. Railway companies built new towns like Wolverton. Francis Head visited it in 1849 and described it as

> a little red brick town composed of 242 little red brick houses—all running either this way or that, all right angles, three or four tall red-brick engine chimneys, a number of very large red brick workshops, six red houses for offices, one red beershop, two red public houses and, we are glad to add, a substantial red schoolroom and a neat stone church, the whole lately built by order of a Railway Board at a railway station by a railway contractor for railwaymen, railway women and railway children.
>
> *Stokers and Pokers, or the London and North Western Railway, 1849*

Crewe became one of the most important of all railway towns. In 1841 only 203 people lived there: by 1901 it had a population of 42,074.

The railway station became a very important place in towns and villages. Fresh food, newspapers and letters travelling by the new penny post (which started in 1840) arrived there. Railways transformed holidaymaking. In 1841 Thomas Cook organised the first of many holiday outings by rail. He joined a gathering of people in Leicester who were planning an outing to a nearby town.

> I proposed that in connection with the meeting to be held in Loughborough in July 1841, a special train should be engaged to take friends from Leicester to Loughborough, a distance of eleven miles. The idea was greatly applauded by the assembly and the next day I applied to the Midlands Railway authorities for a special train, the charge per passenger to be one shilling for the double journey. This was cordially agreed to and on the day proposed 500 passengers were conveyed in 24 open carriages.
> *Jubilee Celebrations at Leicester and Market Harborough*, 1886

From this small start Thomas Cook built up a huge business. Others copied him. Railway outings to places on the coast and in the country were soon very common.

1   Name two ways in which railways changed towns and cities.

81 Another way of getting about: penny-farthing bicycles

82 Building the Metropolitan underground railway in London

Other kinds of travel

Between 1850 and 1900 cycling became very popular. Cycles were uncomfortable at first, but gradually inventors designed all the improvements that make up a modern bicycle. Cycling in the nineteenth century was very peaceful.

> One skimmed along almost without effort. The roads were clear. There were waggons which lumbered along, vast haywains with a fragrant load which you could smell because petrol fumes did not pollute the air. There was a good deal of dust but nobody minded that. There would be peace all around, no noise of grinding machinery, no roar and explosions from motor bikes.
>
> W. Macqueen-Pope, *Give Me Yesterday*, 1957

83 An electric tram in Aberdeen

In 1863 the world's first underground railway opened in London. It was called the Metropolitan Line. Steam locomotives pulled the first trains, filling the tunnels with clouds of smoke. A railwayman who worked on the Underground in its steam days recalled,

> My admission to serve on the District Railway was a thrilling adventure. I was engaged as a Signal Box Boy at a salary of six shillings a week. Hours of duty were nine till seven p.m. I entered the District Railway Service years before electrification and in the tunnels steam and sulphur were the order of the day. The Locomotives were small and powerful. They had no cabs, only a weatherboard.
>
> *Give Me Yesterday*, 1957

By 1900 electric engines pulled many Underground trains. Trams also used electricity. The first trams ran along rails in the streets, pulled by horses. After 1890 most trams used electricity.

Very occasionally, after 1895, the splutter and roar of a motor car began to disturb people's lives.

1 Draw a picture of a penny farthing bicycle.
2 In what ways would it be harder to ride and less comfortable than a modern bicycle?
3 Look at Picture 83. In what ways is the tram different from a modern double-decker bus?
4 Look at Picture 84. The owner of this car must have been very proud of it. Write a letter from him to a friend, telling him or her about it.

9 Soldiers of the Queen

Becoming a soldier

The British soldier of the nineteenth century lived in uncomfortable conditions, ate poor food and received low pay. Yet skilful recruiting officers managed to tempt men to join up for this hard life. This is how one man, Edwin Mole, was persuaded to join the army in 1863. He went one lunchtime with a friend

to a public house on Charles Street, Westminster, much frequented by recruiting sergeants. I remained there for the best part of the afternoon, Sergeant Gibb being very liberal in filling my glass as soon as it was empty. He suggested we should go to his quarters for a cup of tea. To pass the time he began showing me several pictures of soldiers in different army uniforms. Then, pointing to his own regiment, he observed,

'But after all there's none to beat this one in the Service! I think you'd look a rare treat in stable dress.'

I asked him what 'stable' dress was and he said the walking-out costume consisting of dark blue jacket, overalls cut tight to show off the figure to advantage, wellington boots, with a small cap and a whip. As he reeled off the description I could not help comparing it with the clothes I was wearing and he spoke in such a friendly fascinating way that I blurted out 'I've often thought of enlisting.'

'I knew you had,' he said, 'by the smart way you hold yourself. See here,' he went on, 'just step under this and I'll take your height.'

He found I was just the proper height and then began telling me about himself and what he had seen away in Kalapoosh (which was army slang for India) describing his battles in the Mutiny.

'Why lad, you've only to enlist and once your chum claps eyes on you in the Hussar uniform there's nothing'll stop him coming after you. And you'll never want money in the 14th Hussars. If you only keep yourself smart you'll get your fun and plenty of drink free, for the girls will fight for you. The 14th,' he added with a wink of his eye and a cock of his hand, 'get the pick of the girls wherever they go.'

It was arranged we should go to the theatre. We returned, drinks were called for and what with one thing

85 'Who'll serve the Queen?'

109

and what with another I was enticed into taking a drop too much and never rightly remember what happened.

Next morning when I awoke my head was very lumpy. The first thing I saw was Sergeant Gibb sitting up in bed smoking.

'Hello,' he cried, 'You've woke, have you! You'll have to go before the doctor this morning and as it's rather late I think you had better get up at once.'

'What have I to go to the doctor for?'

'Why, you listed last night, of course, and there's the medical to pass. You're a soldier now. If you feel in your pocket you'll find the bob [shilling].'

> *A King's Hussar*, 1893, quoted in R. Palmer,
> *The Rambling Soldier*, 1977

Edwin Mole was in the Hussars for 25 years. Some of his fellow soldiers joined in the hope of finding adventure. Others joined because they had no other work. But many parents did not want their sons to become privates in the army. In 1877 William Robertson joined. He had done well at his Leicestershire village school and his father was a tailor. William's mother heard the news and wrote to him,

There are plenty of things Steady Young Men can do when they can write and read as you can. The army is a refuge for all idle people. I shall name it to no-one for I am ashamed to think of it. I would rather Bury you than see you in a red coat.

> Quoted in A. Ramsay Skelley,
> *The Victorian Army at Home*, 1977

The new recruits trained to be soldiers. This is how J. Macmullen, a soldier who joined in the 1840s, spent his first weeks in the army.

I rose at 5 o'clock in the morning and made up my bed. At six we turned out for drill from which we were dismissed at a quarter to eight when we breakfasted. From ten till twelve we were again at drill, had dinner at one in the shape of potatoes and meat, both usually of the most wretched quality, and at two fell in for another drill which terminated at four after which my time was at my own disposal until tattoo. I generally amused myself by strolling or by reading.

> *Camp and Barrack Room, or the British Army as it is*,
> 1846, quoted in *The Rambling Soldier*, 1977

Even in the later nineteenth century army training was very unsatisfactory. When Robert Blatchford joined he grumbled,

We were only boys but we could see the defects in the Army. We said that the men were not taught to shoot, that

110

86 Troops marching through Gravesend before embarking for foreign service (1846)

not one man in five hundred could use a bayonet effectively, that the officers did not take their work seriously and did not even know the drill-book drill, that we had no practice in making trenches, that scouting was not known and that too much time was wasted on mere pageantry, marching past and other nonsense. Take the dress. Scarlet and pipeclay and brass. Ask any man who has been out for a week's manoeuvres in wet weather what happened to him. An hour's heavy rain washed the pipeclay off the belts all over the scarlet cloth. The buckles made dark stains on the tunic. One good drenching for an hour meant three or four days' hard work.

A Fusilier buckled and belted up tight in a scarlet tunic with straps under his armpits, knapsack, folded coat and canteen on his back, with a great fur balloon on his head was a noble mark for an enemy's fire and could not have shot straight himself if he had been an angel.

My Life in the Army, 1870, quoted in
The Rambling Soldier, 1977

V. 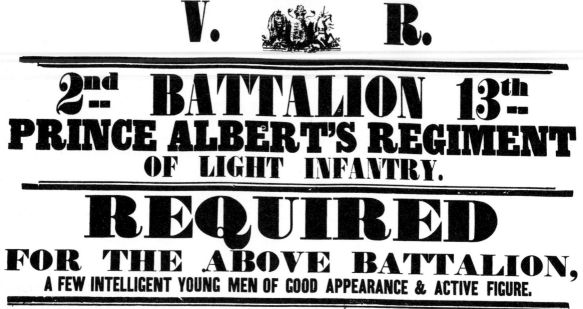 R.

2ⁿᵈ BATTALION 13ᵗʰ
PRINCE ALBERT'S REGIMENT
OF LIGHT INFANTRY.

REQUIRED
FOR THE ABOVE BATTALION,
A FEW INTELLIGENT YOUNG MEN OF GOOD APPEARANCE & ACTIVE FIGURE.

The history of the 13th Light Infantry is so well known in the annals of our countrys' glory, that it would be needless to describe, at any length, the varied scenes, climes, and countries in which, by its gallantry and devoted bravery, it has added to the stability and welfare of the British Empire, " on which the sun never sets."

Under the burning Sun, and on the sandy deserts of the **Land** of the **Egyptians,** in the tropical climate of the **Carribean Sea,** where the Emerald waves roll o'er the golden sands and glittering coral reefs of the **Isle of Martinique ;** in the "Indian Hemisphere," that **Koh-i-noor** of England's Crown, in **Ava, Afghanistan, Ghuznee, Jellalabad,** and **Cabul;** in the glorious **CRIMEAN Campaign ;** and at a later date serving a second time in India, avenging the fell cruelties of the murderous Sepoys ; have waved in victorious triumph the Battle Flags of this Renowned Regiment ! ! !

HONOURS, PROMOTIONS, REWARDS, & IMMENSE SUMS OF PRIZE MONEY FELL TO THE LOT OF THESE HEROES.

THE SPHINX ! !

Emblem of that land where those wonders of all ages, the stupendous Pyramids, raise their undecaying summits to the arch of Heaven.

THE MURAL CROWN!!

Awarded (as in the days of ancient Rome) for deeds of valour, and acts of undying fame, at the heroic defence of the City of **Jellalabad,** a marvel of bravery that sheds a lustre even on the name of Briton ! ! !

With other mottoes and Badges of victorious combat, and emblazoned on the Banners of the Regiment, sparkling like jewels in the sun as the breeze gently fans the silken folds.

TO PERPETUATE ITS FAME TO FUTURE GENERATIONS, HER MAJESTY, THE QUEEN HAS BEEN PLEASED TO BESTOW ON THE CORPS THE PROUD TITLE OF

PRINCE ALBERT'S REGIMENT of Lt. Inft.

And in the presence of assembled thousands, His Royal Highness, the **Prince Consort** presented to the **2nd Battalion** the Colours under which they have now the honour to serve. As a mark of the estimation in which the 2nd Battalion 13th Light Infantry is held. Her Majesty, during the past month, has granted a Commission to the Serjeant Major of the Corps.

From the salubrity of the climate and its even temperature, in addition to the advantages of increased allowances, the Isle of France or Mauritius has been selected as the Station for a few years of the Battalion. It will be recollected that this Isle of the Eastern Ocean is celebrated as the scene of the romantic and interesting narrative of the lives of **Paul** and **Virginie,** and their sad and untimely end.

N.B.—It is advisable that Volunteers for this Battalion should present themselves for Enlistment without delay, as the few present vacancies will be rapidly filled, and thus may be lost an opportunity for travel and observation of the striking scenes of foreign life seldom offered to the aspiring Soldier.

Fermoy, March, 1864.

GOD SAVE THE QUEEN.

1 Find and list three reasons for joining up that Sergeant Gibb offered Edwin Mole.
2 Do you think that any of Sergeant Gibb's reasons were good arguments for joining up? Give a reason for your answer.
3 Explain in your own words why William Robertson's mother did not want him to join the army.
4 Read J. Macmullen's story. Now make up the timetable that might have been pinned up in his barracks to show recruits how their day was organised.
5 What do you think the officer in Picture 85 is saying? Write out the speech that he might be making.
6 Look at Picture 87. Now make up your own recruiting poster to persuade men to join up.

Army life

Soldiers lived in barracks that were very crowded. By morning the air in them was so foul that, as an army sergeant complained,

> If I went in out of my own room sometimes I would not bear it till I had ordered the windows opened to make a draught. I have often retired to the passage and called to the orderly man to open the windows. The air was offensive, both from the men's breath and from urine tubs in the room, and of course some soldiers do not keep their feet clean, especially in summertime.
>
> *Report of the Army Sanitary Commission, 1857–58*

William Robertson joined the army in 1877. He found that there were many things to complain about. The army had recently decided to allow soldiers' wives to live in buildings separate from the general barracks.

> It had been the custom for a married soldier and his wife and children to live in one corner of the barrack room, screened off with blankets, and in return for this accommodation and a share of the rations the wife kept the room clean, washed and mended the men's underclothing and attended to the preparation of their meals.
>
> The barrack room arrangements for sleeping and eating could not be classed as luxurious. The blankets were seldom if ever washed, clean sheets were issued once a month and clean straw for the mattresses once every three months. Besides the beds the only other furniture consisted of four benches and two tables. Plates and basins (paid for by the mess) were the only crockery, the basin being used in turn as a coffee cup, tea cup, beer mug, soup plate, shaving mug and receptacle for pipeclay with which to clean gloves and belts.
>
> The food provided free consisted of one pound of bread

88 The cooking-house of the 8th Hussars during the Crimean War

and three quarters of a pound of meat and nothing more of any kind. Green vegetables and all other requirements were paid for by the men, who had a daily deduction of 3½ pence made from their pay of one shilling and two pence for that purpose. The regular meals were coffee and bread for breakfast, meat and potatoes for dinner, with soup or pudding once or twice a week, tea and bread for tea.

From Private to Field Marshal, 1921

When Robertson joined up in 1877 army life was in fact improving! A few years earlier 4½ pence was stopped from soldiers' pay for the meat and bread. But the pay was still very low. A private earned only £18–£25 a year—before stoppages. Money was taken from his wages to pay for hot water for washing, for haircuts, and for damage to barrack-room furniture. The soldier ate poor food and drank tea that the cooks brewed in greasy potato pots.

The soldier who misbehaved suffered fierce punishments. Until 1881 officers could order soldiers to be flogged with a whip. A soldier might suffer as many as 200 lashes until, in 1856, after the death of several men, the number permitted was cut to fifty. Alexander Somerville was flogged. Two men took turns to beat him with a whip made of several leather strands called a 'cat o' nine tails'.

I felt an astounding sensation between the shoulders, under my neck, which went to my toe nails in one direction, my finger nails in another, and stung me to the heart as if a knife had gone through my body. The sergeant major called in a loud voice, 'One'. The time between each stroke seemed so long as to be agonising and yet the next came too soon. 'Five', 'Six' followed, so on up to twenty-five. The sergeant major then said 'Halt'. A young trumpeter who had not flogged before took his cat and began. He gave me some dreadful cuts about the ribs, first one side, and then on the other. It now became Simpson's turn to give twenty-five. I felt as if I had lived all the time of my real life in pain and torture.

The Autobiography of a Working Man, 1848, quoted in *The Rambling Soldier*, 1977

'Field Punishment Number One' replaced flogging in 1881. The man being punished was lashed to a gunwheel for many hours.

89 A military flogging

1 Give two reasons why barrack room air was so foul.
2 How much a day was an ordinary soldier paid?
3 Why did he not actually get all of this wage?
4 Using William Robertson's description, make up a menu board for one day's meals, to be placed outside the cookhouse.

5 Imagine you are one of the two drummer boys in Picture 89. Write to your parents telling them about what you have seen. Mention how the man was tied up, how he was punished and how the other soldiers watching him behaved.

Officers

Most officers in the Victorian Army were men with private incomes. Until 1871 they had to pay for their positions. This is what it cost to buy commissions in the Foot Guards in 1840:

Lieutenant   £2,050
Captain   £4,800
General   £8,300

After 1871 officers still needed money of their own. They had to buy costly uniforms and pay for food and for much of their equipment. Their pay was not high. In an ordinary infantry regiment a second lieutenant received 4/6 a day up to 1856, then 5/3. Even a lieutenant colonel was paid only 18/-. Some officers were elderly. In the Crimean War the chief engineer, Sir John Burgoyne, was in his seventies.

Few ordinary soldiers rose above the rank of sergeant. The most famous private to be promoted was William Robertson. When he joined up in 1877 only six out of every hundred lieutenants came from the ranks. When he finally left the army, Robertson had risen to the highest rank of all—he was a field marshal.

He found his early years very lonely. When he first became a lieutenant he didn't dare join the other officers for dinner on his first night. He wrote home,

> The officers who now know me are very nice but it is a difficult business, you see I feel I am acting under a false flag if they do not know my previous life. I find that the clothes Father made for me compare very favourably with any others here and feel very thankful for the trouble he has taken and hope to repay him one day. Have not got into eating about eight courses at night. Of course I should like a bit more companionship during my walks but that will come in time, anyway it doesn't matter as I do not care much for it.

When Robertson first went to join the army in India he wrote home,

> It is so miserable out here you don't know, I'm afraid I do not remember how often I must feel cut off from all friendship; sincere mutual interest cannot naturally be between a born gentleman and one who is only now beginning to try to become one.
>
> Quoted in B. Farwell, *For Queen and Country*, 1981

1 Why was Robertson lucky that his father was a tailor?
2 Why do you think he found eight course dinners in the evening a struggle to manage?
3 What do you think an officer from a wealthy family who didn't like Robertson might have said to him in order to hurt his feelings?

At war

The Victorian Army was often at war. British soldiers served all over the world, winning and controlling a huge empire. One of the most serious wars was against Russia in 1854–6. The British Government thought that Russia was trying to weaken Britain's Empire. Britain sent troops to fight alongside French and Turkish soldiers in a part of southern Russia called the Crimea.

Among the men who sailed to fight in this war was Lieutenant Colonel S. J. G. Calthorpe. He was the nephew of the commander, Lord Raglan. His letters show what the war was like.

> We left on April 8th 1854 at 9 a.m., the band of the Royal Artillery playing us off to the tune of 'Cheer boys, cheer'. It was curious to watch the countenances [faces] of the soldiers, some faces so full of hope and glowing with excitement, others so sad and dejected that one wondered

90 The Crimean War

how they could cheer so lustily. Almost 3 weeks later we steamed into the Bosphorus, following calls at Gibraltar and Malta. On the morning of the 25th April we landed at Scutari. Everything appeared in the greatest confusion.

At a quarter to 5 a.m., (September 10th) we first caught sight of Sebastopol. We remained for upwards of half an hour gazing at the scene before us with an interest deeply excited by the thought that there lay the prize for which we were to fight. The fortification looked of immense strength and appeared to bristle with guns.

The British and French defeated a Russian attempt to stop them at the Alma River. But there were other dangers.

There is still, I am sorry to say, a great deal of cholera in the army. The casualties from it are daily twelve or fourteen deaths and from thirty to forty fresh cases brought into hospital.

The hospitals were not in the most comfortable state but great excuses are to be made: the weather, the difficulty of getting the bedding cleaned, the dreadful disorder from which most of the patients are suffering [cholera].

Extracts taken from *Cadogan's Crimea*, 1979, first published 1856

It was these dreadful hospital conditions that Florence Nightingale and her nurses tackled so bravely and successfully. British troops were getting the appalling medical care that had long been usual in the army. But this time William Russell of *The Times* was on the spot. His reports stirred a storm of protest at home. He wrote,

Not only are there not sufficient surgeons, not only are there no nurses, there is not even linen to make bandages. Not only are the men kept, in some cases for a week without the hand of a medical man coming near their wounds, not only are they left to expire in agony, but the commonest appliances of a workhouse sick ward are wanting and the men must die through the medical staff of the British Army having forgotten that old rags are necessary for the dressing of wounds.

Quoted in C. Woodham Smith, *Florence Nightingale*, 1950

The Allies did not attack Sebastopol at once. Lieutenant Colonel Calthorpe continued,

The Russian engineers set to work in earnest and large batteries were constructed on every available spot that did

in any way assist the defence of the place. When we first set down before Sevastopol we saw thousands of men employed making earthworks.

The Russians tried to drive away their attackers. The result was the Battle of Balaclava, 25 October 1854.

The enemy's cavalry now began to advance across the valley in the direction of the English and Turkish troops in line under the command of Sir Colin Campbell. The Turks fired a harmless volley then ran. The Russians came on with a rush yelling in a very barbarous manner. The British soldiers gave them their first volley which checked both their pace and noise. Volley number two then rang out. This was enough for the Ruskies.

The British Heavy Brigade cavalry successfully charged the Russian cavalry. Then followed a disaster. The Light Brigade was given confused orders by a messenger, Captain Nolan. It set off, led by Lord Cardigan.

To the horror of all of us on the height above we saw our handful of light cavalry advance towards the Russian batteries' heavy guns. Poor Nolan galloped some way ahead,

92 *This cartoon shows Lord Cardigan and his men charging the Russian guns at Balaclava*

waving his sword and encouraging his men. Before they had gone any distance the enemy's guns opened on them at long range. Nolan was the first man killed; some grapeshot hit him in the chest; his horse turned and carried him to the rear through our advancing squadrons. His screams were heard far above the din of battle and he fell dead from his saddle near the spot where the order had been given for the charge. The pace of our cavalry increased every moment. On they went headlong to death. At length they arrived at the guns, the few that remained made fearful havoc among the enemy's artillerymen.

Only about a quarter of the Light Brigade survived.

At Inkerman the Russians again tried to drive away the Allies.

On Sunday November 5th 1854 we had another awful battle. The morning was foggy. It was 5.30 a.m. when one of the pickets of the Light Division saw the Russian infantry.

When the Russians finally retreated they left a fearful scene.

Mangled corpses of friend and foe lay in every direction: such heaps of slain. In some places down the Inkerman road where our shot and shell had fallen into the retreating columns of the enemy, the way was blocked up with dead and dying.

In September 1855 the British and French troops launched fierce attacks on Sebastopol. They captured it only after suffering terrible losses as they tried to clamber into the forts that protected the town. This is how Calthorpe described an attack on a fort called the 'Redan'.

Immediately after General Simpson put up the signal for the advance the English rushed over the parapets and advanced towards the Redan. The ladder and storming parties dashed on in a very gallant manner under a heavy fire and the foremost got over the ditch, up the parapet and in with wonderful rapidity. But there, poor fellows, they only met with a soldiers' death. The storming parties still continued to arrive. The enemy poured a most galling fire upon the angle where the British troops were assembled, numbers of the poor fellows were dropping, killed or wounded, every instant. The few untouched men left in the Redan were driven out by the mass of Russians which charged down upon them. The assault on the Redan was given up.

93 The defeat of the Russians at Inkerman

Cadogan's Crimea, 1979, first published 1856

In September 1855 the Russians finally left Sebastopol. Months of furious fighting and of suffering in cold, muddy and unhealthy conditions led up to the victory.

1 Design a recruiting poster to persuade men to fight in the Crimean War.
2 What were the two main battles in the war?
3 The Allies did not attack Sebastopol at once. How did the Russians use the time given them by this delay?
4 What do you imagine the Russian artillery commander thought about the charge of the Light Brigade? Imagine you are the commander. Write a report for your general.

Changes in the army

The Crimean War was followed by a number of changes in the army. By 1900 army life had improved. Some of the most important changes were carried out in 1870 by the Secretary for War, Edward Cardwell. He allowed men to join the army for just a few years. He increased pay. He organised regiments into two battalions each, and named them after the different parts of Britain where they were based. Previously they had simply been given numbers.

His changes were not always popular. When Colonel Charles Poole of the 67th Foot was asked to dine with his regiment (now renamed the Hampshires), he wrote,

> Since time immemorial regiments have been numbered according to their precedence in the line. Nothing can alter the rightness of such a plan and interfering boobies in the War Office can have no effect on my determination to ignore their damned machinery at all costs to myself. I will not come to anything called a Hampshire Regimental Dinner,
> My compliments, Sir, and be damned.
> Quoted in *For Queen and Country*, 1981

Physical exercise training was added to the drilling. When Robert Blatchford joined he was faced with this:

> It was very cold when we turned out for our first recruits' drill at six o'clock one morning. A short red-headed crabby gymnastic sergeant came and looked us over, after which a corporal formed us into fours and led us on a run of 1,000 yards round a field. This over we went to dumb bells and parallel bars, very funny were some of the attempts made by the raw boys who had never seen a gymnasium before.
> *My life in the Army*, 1870

The government provided better barracks, better food, separate homes for soldiers' wives and schooling for the men. If privates wanted to become corporals or sergeants they had to pass tests. Greville Murray was a soldier in 1882. He described an army class.

> Here were the forms for beginners who could neither read nor write—fearful dolts some of them who bleated through their spelling most ruefully. Then came a class which contained several middle-aged corporals who had got a third class certificate but were trying to qualify for sergeantships by getting second classes. Some of these unfortunates, who were splendid soldiers, fairly sweated over the difficulties of compound interest. The big drops stood on their foreheads and there was a dazed frown between their eyes as they tried to comprehend the patient demonstration of their teacher expounding to them that $\frac{1}{2}$ and $\frac{6}{12}$ meant the same thing.
>
> *Six Months in the Ranks*, 1882,
> quoted in *The Victorian Army At Home*, 1977

Some soldiers began to think that it would be sensible if troops changed their red uniforms for a colour the enemy would not spot so easily. In 1883 the Commander in Chief wrote to *The Times*,

> I should be sorry to see the day when the English Army is no longer in red. I am not of those who think it at all desirable to hide ourselves too much. I must say I think the soldier had better be taught not to hide himself but to go gallantly to the front. In action the man who does that has a much better chance of succeeding than the man who hides himself.

Nevertheless by 1901 British troops wore khaki when in action.

1 List three improvements made in the army after 1856.
2 Write a letter in reply to the Commander in Chief's defence of red uniforms.

10 Criminals and Police

Different sorts of criminals

Britain's towns and cities contained many criminals. The newspaper journalist Henry Mayhew was determined to find out more about them. One evening in 1864 he went to a very unusual meeting. A number of criminals had gathered in a London schoolroom. A chairman spoke to the meeting.

> The announcement that the greater number present were thieves pleased them exceedingly and was received with three rounds of applause. The announcements in reply to the questions as to the number of times that any of them had been in prison was received with applause which became boisterous as the number of imprisonments increased. When it was announced that one, although only 19 years of age, had been in prison as many as 29 times, the clapping of hands and shouts of 'brayvo', lasted for several minutes and boys rose to look at the distinguished individual.
>
> H. Mayhew, *London Labour and the London Poor*, 1864

94 *A thieves' gambling den (1870)*

95 *The lady of the house face to face with a dangerous-looking tramp*

Henry Mayhew met many different criminals. He explained that there were several sorts of thieves, including these:

Drag Sneaks — or those who steal goods or luggage from carts or coaches.

Star-glazers — or those who cut the panes out of shop windows.

Till-friskers — or those who empty tills during the absence of shopkeepers.

Noisy Racket Men — or those who steal china or glass from outside china shops.

Dead Lurkers — or those who steal coats and umbrellas at dusk or on Sunday afternoons.

Mudlarks — or those who steal pieces of rope and lumps of coal from among the vessels at the river-side.

96 A cartoon in Punch *magazine suggested this sort of clothing would protect the wearer from garotters*

Mayhew reported that there were even more dangerous criminals lurking in London's streets.

> Robberies are also effected by garotting, frequently on foggy nights. A ruffian walks up and throws his arm round the neck of a person who has a watch or whom he has noticed carrying money. The garotter tries to get his arm under his chin. He does it so violently the man is almost strangled and is unable to cry out. He holds him in this position while his companions rifle his pockets.

Children who lived in very poor homes were often tempted to steal. Arthur Harding was brought up in a London slum. He remembered,

> Children would steal from the coal vans. It was something that made a mother happy when a child brought something home, instead of a bashing they'd get an extra lump of pudding at dinner. If somebody on the first floor said 'Bring me up a bag of coal' the coalman would have to go up and that left the van at the mercy of the street urchins. Pinching things from vans was easy. They'd go at a slow pace—8 to 10 m.p.h.—and a lot of goods were taken by barrow.
> Quoted in R. Samuel (ed.) *East End Underworld*, 1981

The most famous Victorian criminal was never caught. In 1888 he killed at least five women in a poor part of London called

Whitechapel. This is how *The Illustrated Police News*, 8 September 1888, reported one of his crimes.

> At a quarter to four on Friday morning P.C. Neil was on his beat in Bucks Row, Thomas St., Whitechapel, when his attention was attracted by the body of a woman lying on the pavement. Bucks Row, like many other minor thoroughfares in this neighbourhood is not overburdened with gas lamps and at first the constable thought the woman had fallen down in a drunken stupor. With the aid of the light from his lantern Neil perceived the woman had been the victim of some horrible outrage. The murdered woman is about 45 years of age. The mark 'Lambeth Workhouse' was found stamped on the petticoat.

On 28 September the Central News Agency received a note. It read,

> I keep on hearing the police have caught me, but they won't fix me just yet. I have laughed when they look so clever and talk about being on the right track. Jack the Ripper.
> *The Illustrated Police News*, 1888

The murderer killed with a type of knife used by surgeons. He mutilated his victims horribly. He was never caught, yet suddenly the crimes stopped. Even today people still argue about who he might have been.

1 What sort of trickster is shown in Picture 95?
2 Can you think of other words to describe him, like those in Mayhew's list?
3 Choose one of Mayhew's names for thieves. Explain why you think it is a very suitable name for the sort of thief to whom it refers.
4 What sort of housing area do you think lay around the schoolroom where the thieves met?
5 The people at the meeting had been sent tickets of invitation. Design the sort of ticket you think might have been used.
6 Imagine you are PC Neil. Write a report for your inspector.

The new police

The modern police force began in 1829 in the City of London. Until the nineteenth century all sorts of people acted as policemen. Badly paid night-watchmen kept guard in some towns at times when criminals were busiest. In other places unpaid constables did the job. Men were made to take turns at it. This led to some unsuitable appointments. In 1839 *The Aylesbury News* reported,

> At Chesham there is a smith appointed constable, thief-taker and peace officer who has been publicly flogged in the

127

97 A night-watchman

98 The new policemen

town of Chesham, once privately flogged at Aylesbury Gaol, once convicted of stealing lead, and once committed to hard labour for assaulting and robbing a boy.

Unpaid constables and elderly night-watchmen could not possibly control all the criminals in towns and cities. Sir Robert Peel set up a London police force who wore uniforms and were paid reasonable wages. Britain's other cities copied London. By 1857 the government insisted that full-time police forces should be set up throughout the country.

Many British people were very suspicious of the police at first. Police uniforms were carefully designed not to look like soldiers' uniforms, and the policemen usually carried only sticks as weapons. Detective forces were not set up at first for fear that people would think the detectives were government spies. London's detective force was founded in 1842. Its offices were behind the main Whitehall Place police offices, just off Scotland

Yard. By 1867 there were still only fifteen detectives at Scotland Yard.

The dark blue uniform of the police was heavy to wear, as a former policeman remembered in 1855.

> I had to put on a swallow-tail coat and a rabbit-skin high top hat covered with leather weighing 18 ounces: a pair of Wellington boots, a belt with a great brass buckle. My hat was slipping all over my head, my boots, which were two sizes too large, were rubbing the skin off my heels.
>
> Quoted in J. Wilkes,
> *The London Police in the Nineteenth Century*, 1977

The man in charge of a police force might come from a well-to-do family. Ordinary policemen were recruited from the working class. A man wishing to join the police had to be able to read, write and do simple arithmetic. He had to be under 35 years old and at least 5 feet 8 inches tall.

This is how much the police were paid a year.

Constable	£54	Inspector	£100
Sergeant	£58	Superintendent	£200

It was not very much. A skilled craftsman earned about the same as an Inspector. Policemen had to work seven days a week, walk about twenty miles a day and, until 1900, they had no official time off. But at least they had regular pay and a chance of promotion. These orders of 1842 for the Lancashire police show that it was not easy for men to behave as policemen were expected to behave.

99 *An arrest at a lodging house*

Nothing degrades a police constable so much as drunkenness, nothing reflects so much discredit upon the Force, nor is any other fault so soon observed by the Public: no individual, even although he may not be on duty at the time shall frequent [go to] Public Houses. If a constable needs refreshment he must have it conveyed to his home.

Good temper is almost as essential. A constable is constantly exposed to numerous insults. Neither resentment nor anger is becoming to him. The more civil and respectful the Police, the more will they be supported by the public.

Lancashire Record Office, 1842

100 *The turnip stealers*

Many constables were dismissed, like this London policeman of 1862 whose name appeared in an official list.

> Dismissals—P.C. 466 Turner: drunk on duty, losing his truncheon and 3 keys belonging to premises, and complained of by two civilians for assaulting them with his rattle.

(Until 1884 the police carried large wooden rattles instead of whistles.)

Constables were often tempted to drink alcohol. Public houses were open all day and some of them drank large quantities of beer (often because it was very difficult to find anything else). Some constables became very weary during their long hours of duty. One of them wrote a letter to *The Daily Telegraph* in 1865 to say that a policeman

> gets tired and careless of his duties and instead of looking out for thieves is dividing his time between glasses of ale, inspectors, drops of something short [spirits], sergeants, bits of cold mutton and superintendents.

1 Is the night-watchman in Picture 97 well prepared to deal with criminals? What has he got to help him do his job?
2 In this section you can find reasons for joining the police and some information about the sort of person who was needed. Design a poster to try to persuade people to join the police.
3 Imagine you have just been dismissed from the police. Write a letter to your parents explaining how you came to be dismissed and why you are not sorry to be leaving.

A famous detective

One of the most successful Victorian detectives was James McLevy. For thirty years he served the City of Edinburgh, first as a night-watchman, then—until 1860—as a detective. He claimed,

> I can always tell an unlucky thief from a lucky one, one with full fobs from one with empty pockets, one who suspects being scented from one who is on the scent.

He thought his success was due to careful observation.

> People give McLevy praise for some extraordinary powers. It is all nonsense. My deductions have been, and are, very simple pieces of business.

He spent a lot of time wandering around the places that he knew criminals went to. At certain public houses and lodging houses he often found stolen goods. He wrote,

101 Edinburgh in about 1870

Among these there was the *Cock and Trumpet*. On one occasion I issued triumphantly with a cheese weighing 30 pounds, on another with a dozen sausages and on another with 2 live geese. The landlady never knew that such things were in her house.

He found one thief, with stolen hens and ducks,

plucking lustily at the fowls. He had finished 9 hens and was busy with the last of 9 ducks. 'What a fine show of poultry, Sandy now,' said I, 'Where got you so many hens and ducks?' Replied the rogue, 'They flew in at the window.'

McLevy knew many criminals by sight. For years he had been trying to catch a thief called Adam McDonald. One day he saw him, with a friend called Chisholm, taking a drunk called Kerr down a dark alley. He remembered what happened with pleasure.

In an instant the feet were taken from Kerr, he was thrown flat on his back with a sound of his head on the granite. Chisholm held him down, Adam whirling his gold chain over the victim's head, rolled it up in his hand along with the watch and bolted. But whither did Adam bolt? Into my very arms! He commenced to struggle with me which, if I had not been of the strength I am, would have ended in his escape, while spluttering, 'McLevy! The devil of all devils!'
The Casebook of a Victorian Detective, 1975

1 What made McLevy such a good detective?

2 Imagine you are either Sandy or Adam in the above stories. You are telling a friend who is visiting you in prison how you planned and carried out a crime, but were caught by McLevy.

Punishments

During the nineteenth century the government struggled to find ways of dealing with the large numbers of criminals who were caught. There were not many large prisons at the beginning of the Victorian period. Until the 1850s judges often sent convicts to work in one of Britain's colonies. Thousands were sent out to Australia, Tasmania, Gibraltar or Bermuda. Although these convicts were separated from their friends and families, some eventually did quite well in their new life. One of them, Richard Taylor, wrote home to his father from New South Wales in 1851.

> I was assigned to the Hospital where I had 39 fellows one of whom was a boot and shoe maker and I eventually picked up the trade by which I earn a comfortable living. I live in my little property, it is only half an acre but it faces the road where the gold coach passes. I married my wife when she was a fellow 'servant', two of my children goes to school every day. Tell my brother good tradesmen can earn from one to two guineas a week and provisions are much cheaper here, this is the land of plenty and perpetual summer.
>
> Lancashire Record Office

Many criminals were executed. The crimes for which it was possible to be executed included these:

> High treason, murder, administering of poison with intent to murder, causing injury with intent to murder, robbery accompanied with wounding, burglary accompanied with an intent to murder or wounding or striking any person being in their dwelling house, setting fire to a dwelling house—any person being therein.
>
> Parliamentary Debates, 1864

102 Crowds gathering to watch an execution at Newgate prison (1848)

Some criminals were hanged in public. Large numbers of people gathered to watch. On 15 November 1864, *The Times* reported the execution of a man named Muller.

> Yesterday morning Muller was hung in front of Newgate. Until about 3 o'clock not more than some 4,000, or at most 5,000 were assembled. Then, as every minute the day broke more and more clear the crowd could be seen in all the horrible reality in which it had been heard throughout the long wet night.
> At last, near 8 o'clock, there came shouts of 'Hats off!' and

the whole mass commenced, amidst cries and struggles, to wriggle to and fro as the bell of Newgate began to toll. The prisoner was escorted to the scaffold. Following him close came the common hangman who at once pulling a white cap over the condemned man's face, fastened his feet with a strap and shambled off the scaffold amid low hisses. The drop fell. Muller had ceased to live. For five or ten minutes the crowd were awed and stilled by this quiet, rapid passage from life to death. The impression did not last for long, robbery and violence, loud laughing, oaths, fighting, reigned around the gallows.

In 1868 the government decided that in future hangings were to be carried out inside prison walls.

1 Can you see any clue in the picture that suggests that watching a hanging was thought of as a popular entertainment?
2 Do you think people of the time could have thought of any serious reason in favour of public hangings?

Prisons

During the nineteenth century many new prisons were built in Britain. Until 1850, however, hundreds of men were housed in old warships called 'hulks'. In 1847 a group of MPs visited five hulks anchored at Woolwich. They reported,

The men sleep in hammocks. Prisoners work in the dock-yards. In the hospital ship 'Unite' the great majority of the patients were infested with vermin and their persons begrimed with dirt, many men had been 5 weeks without a change, all record had been lost of when the blankets had been washed. A large proportion of the convicts were affected by symptoms of scurvy. Convicts have been whipped with a birch without reference to the Superintendent.

The MPs also noted down the convicts' duties.

At 3.30 a.m. the Quartermaster, accompanied by a Guard, is to unlock the cell where the cooks are confined and let them up to prepare breakfast. At 5.0 a.m. all hands are to be called, the hammocks lowered and made up. At 6.0 breakfast to be served, at 6.30 wards to be swept.
At 7.0 prisoners mustered out to labour in gangs, irons to be examined and prisoners to be searched. At quarter before 12 prisoners are to return on board and be searched, dinner served. At 1.0 the prisoners are to be mustered to labour, searched, and at quarter before 6.0 they return. Each prisoner after washing himself to take his hammock and proceed to his ward. Supper to be served and cells

locked. After prayers prisoners may be allowed to write to their friends.

Parliamentary Papers, 1847, *vol.* 12

The MPs thought that the hulks were not fit for use as prisons.

At about the same time the colonies to which Britain sent convicts were refusing to take any more. The government had to spend money on the building of prisons like Dartmoor and Parkhurst.

The prison officers wanted to keep their prisoners busy but could not always think of useful work for them to do. In 1865 Thomas Archer, who wrote two books on prisons, noted that although

the carpenters, coopers, smiths, and other shops are busy, the prison work in the way of plastering, painting, shoemaking and tailoring is done by convicts and the tin porringers in which food is dispensed are made by the prison tinsmiths, oakum picking is the busiest employment [untangling tarred rope]. The treadmill occupies one side of this room where some hard labour felons are engaged in ascending a sort of revolving paddle box. A revolution of the wheel includes thirtyfour steps. At every 30th revolution a bell announces that the spell of work is finished, a prisoner completes fifteen of these spells in nearly four hours.

The Pauper, the Thief and the Convict, 1865

Some treadmills turned mills that ground corn. Shipbuilders found tarred rope useful. But many prisoners were made to do work that was useless. Prisoners were lined up and had to pass a twenty-four-pound weight up and down. This was called shot drill. Or they might have to turn a very heavy handle called a crank. The only purpose of this work was to tire the men. In 1898 the government decided on

the abolition of the old forms of hard labour—cranks, treadwheels etc., the labour of all prisoners should be productive. Improved methods for the education of prisoners. Improved prison diet, better sanitation, corporal punish-

> ment only as a penalty for gross personal violence to prison officers and for mutiny.
>
> *Prisons Act*, 1898

Some prison governors kept the prisoners completely apart from one another. They hoped it would make them think about the wrong they had done and change their ways. But such loneliness made many prisoners ill. Many governors ran their prisons on the silent system. Prisoners were not allowed to talk to one another. John Clay watched the prisoners working and eating in silence at Preston Prison where he was chaplain.

> No sign, no look, whether of recognition to a fellow prisoner or of curiosity to a visitor is permitted. A prisoner recently committed and not quite sober once started up with the cry 'Britons never shall be slaves!' A quiet smile on the face of some of the old gaol birds was the only result. Not a head was turned.
>
> Quoted in J. Tobias, *Nineteenth-Century Crime: Prevention and Punishment*, 1972

By 1900, although thirteen treadwheels were still working, prisoners were generally given useful work to do. The 'separate' and 'silent' systems had gone. But among the prisoners were many children. Not until 1908 were they separated from adult prisoners, though a start was made in Victorian times. Parkhurst opened as a prison for children. Around the buildings were

> about 80 acres, the land the boys have to cultivate. When a juvenile convict is first sent to Parkhurst he is placed in rigid seclusion for 3 or 4 months, confined in a separate cell, not able to speak to or see, except at chapel, any of his fellow prisoners, and is instructed in tailoring or knitting.
>
> W. H. Dixon, *London Prisons*, 1850

1 List two of the conditions that were unsatisfactory on board the 'Unite'.
2 How many hours' work a day did hulk prisoners do?
3 What do you think the 'irons' were that had to be carefully examined?
4 Why do you think the prisoners had to be searched?
5 Imagine you are either a prisoner on a hulk or one of the children sent to Parkhurst. Write a letter home to tell your family what you do every day and how you feel.

11 Time Off

Time off increased during Victoria's reign. New laws limited the length of the working day, travel became easier, and people had more money to spend. In 1871 Bank Holidays began. Office and bank workers were given certain days as official holidays. A *Times* reporter watched Londoners enjoying their first Bank Holiday.

Cyclists of both sexes covered the roads. River steamers and pleasure boats carried their thousands to Kew and the upper reaches of the Thames. The London parks were crowded. The Botanic Gardens and Zoological Gardens

105 A Victorian public house

formed great attractions and the flowers of Battersea Park drew large crowds.

The Times, August 1871

During the evenings many people visited public houses. Some 'pubs' paid singers to entertain the customers. A visitor to one public house noticed how much the audience enjoyed singing.

At the end of every verse the audience takes up the chorus with a zest and vigour which speaks volumes—they sing, they roar, they yell, they scream, they get on their legs and waving dirty hands and ragged hats, bellow again till their voices crack.

Chambers' Edinburgh Journal, 1856

Some places served food as well as drink. In London, Evans' Supper Rooms were very popular with people who had large appetites.

See the suppers set forth for the strong-stomached supporters of Evans. See the pyramids of dishes arrive, the

106 A 'song and supper room' (1859)

> steaming succession of red-hot chops. See the severe kid-
> neys weltering proudly in their noble gravy. Sniff the frag-
> rant vapour of the corpulent [fat] sausage. Mark how the
> russet leathern-coated baked potato at first defies the knife.
> Pints of stout if you please, no puny half-measures!
>
> G. A. Sava, *Twice the Clock Round*, 1859

As more people came to live in towns and cities, parks, gardens, libraries and museums were provided for them. Street
entertainers wandered about, trying to catch people's attention
and collect their money. Henry Mayhew met two entertainers.
The first, an Italian, owned a bear.

> He used to beat the bear and manage her: they called her
> Jenny. The monkey was dressed the same as a soldier. He
> jumped up and down on the bear. The bear had been
> taught to roll and tumble. We fed her on bread, boiled
> 'tatoes' or raw carrots. Besides them we had two dancing
> dogs. The dogs jumped through hoops and danced on their
> hind legs.

The second man was a fire-eater. He told Mayhew,

> I practised the fire eating at home. It used to make me very
> thick in my voice. It blistered my mouth swallowing the fire
> but I never burnt myself seriously at it. I got travelling with
> a man that swallowed a poker. I wore a kind of scale armour
> costume with a red lion on the breast. I do up my mous-
> tache with cork and rouge a bit. My tights is brown with
> black boots. On my head I wear a king's crown and a ringlet
> wig. I begin eating the lighted link [torch]. Sometimes I
> makes a slip and don't put it in careful, it makes your
> moustache fizz up.
>
> *London Labour and the London Poor*, 1851

1 List at least two ways in which Londoners spent a Bank Holiday.
2 Imagine you are a newspaper reporter. Write an article called 'An
  Evening Out in London'. Describe the sights and sounds of the
  streets, pubs and supper rooms.
3 Draw a picture of the fire-eater, using his description of himself.

Going to a show

All sorts of travelling shows and fairs provided entertainment.
At Ramsay Fair

> You could buy things to eat like hot pies in a basin or a dish
> o' whelks or a packet o' brandy-snaps. There were the Fat
> Lady, all dressed up in spangles, a mountain o' flesh and
> blood, and a couple o' tiny dwarfs called Tom Thumb and
> his wife. In another booth there were conjurers and in

107 *Enjoying a Sunday afternoon (about 1835)*

another the performing fleas. There was the boxing booth and the waxwork show.

Quoted in J. Walvin, *Leisure and Society 1850–1950*, 1978

Travelling animal shows were popular. Francis Kilvert went to one. Afterwards he wrote in his diary (7 May 1872),

Wombwell's Menagerie came into Hay and the elephant was advertised to ride upon a bicycle. Teddy Bevan and I went out to meet the caravans which were looming in the distance. The Elephant, a very small one, and three camels, came shuffling and splashing along the muddy road.

At 6 o'clock the wild beasts were ready and we all went to the show. There was a fair lion and a decent wolf. A laughing hyena set us all off laughing in chorus. A black sheep in the pangs of hunger was bleating piteously. There was no bicycle forthcoming. The ground was in a swamp with pools of water and huge gaps of canvas overhead let in the pouring rain.

W. Plomer (ed.), *Kilvert's Diary, 1870–79*, 1944

108 *A magic lantern show (1858)*

Actors travelled around putting on plays in tents and in halls. One travelling actor told Henry Mayhew,

> It's a jolly life, strolling. At times it's hard lines but for my part I prefer it to any other. It's fifteen shillings a week for certain. If you can make up your mind to sleep in the booth it ain't such bad pay. Mummers' [actors] feed is herring. Mummers is the poorest, flashiest and most independent race of men going. Private business is a better sort of acting. There we do nearly the entire piece with only the difficult parts cut out. We only do the outline of the story and gag it up. We've done various plays of Shakespeare in this way.

Until the early cinema began in the late 1890s, magic lantern shows were popular. Photographs or painted scenes were shone onto a screen using an oil lamp, or a gas light, or—finally—electricity. A showman who owned a lantern told Mayhew,

> A month before Christmas we went with a show of a magic lantern. We showed it on a white sheet or on the ceiling in the houses of the gentlefolk and the schools when they was a-breaking up. It was shown by way of a treat to the scholars. There was Harlequin Billy Button and such like.
> *London Labour and the London Poor*, 1851

Of course there were also proper theatres where shows were held. William Taylor, a footman in a rich family's house, was allowed to go to a pantomime in Drury Lane in 1837. He kept a diary in which he wrote (mis-spelling some words),

> The first part was Sinderella. I saw her in the kitchen among the sinders and saw the old wich turne her into a lady and made a carriage out of a pumpkin, four horses out of white

109 A music hall

mice, a coachman out of a rat. This was done by the stage opening and the real things being pushed up by people below and the rat, mice and pumpkin and things being pulled below at the same time. Saw Sinderella go to the ball and lose her slipper and in the end was married to a Prince. The second part was a pantomime where the clowns and harlequins made a great deal of funn by turning one thing into another such as an old woman into a young one. In this part I saw the Devil in hell. There were more things too numerous to mention. Got to bed by one o'clock.

Quoted in J. Burnett, *Useful Toil*, 1974

People who had lived in the countryside were sometimes rather shocked by these city entertainments. The Whitworth family, who lived in Salford, persuaded their grandmother to go to the pantomime. She came from the countryside and did not like what she saw.

Well, it started and when the ballet came on and there were dancing girls and they'd be in tights, she says to me dad, she said, 'William, take me home.' He said, 'It's only just started, mother.' She said, 'Take me home. I'm not sitting here watching them dancing and kicking their legs about,' she says, 'And wagging their fat tails behind them,' she says, 'the brazen hussies.'

Quoted in H. J. Dyos and M. Wolff,
The Victorian City, Images and Realities, 1973

Victorians were especially fond of music halls. Here there were songs, dances, jokes and entertainers like jugglers and acrobats. Henry Mayhew went to a London music hall. He climbed up to the gallery, where there were

> lads from about twelve to three-and-twenty. Young girls too are very plentiful. The bonnets of the 'ladies' are hung over the iron railing in front and one of the amusements of the lads in the back seats consists in pitching orange peel or nutshells into them.
>
> When the orchestra begins playing before 'the gods' have settled into their seats it is impossible to hear a note of music. Presently a fight is sure to begin and then everyone rises from his seat whistling and shouting. But the commotion ceases suddenly at the rising of the curtain.
>
> The dances and comic songs are liked better than anything else. But the grand hit of the evening is always when a song is sung in which the entire gallery can join in chorus.
>
> *London Labour and the London Poor*, 1851

1 Imagine you are in charge of Ramsey Fair. You have to draw a plan of all the different shows and stalls. Label all the different places.
2 How do you think the man in charge of the menagerie would have announced his show to the people of Hay? Write down what he might have called out to passers-by in the town square to persuade them to come to the show.
3 What sort of impressive title do you think the acrobat in the music hall picture might have given himself?
4 Why did some people like the hard life of a travelling actor?

Taking exercise

During the nineteenth century many of today's popular sports were properly organised for the first time. The rules for Rugby Union were drawn up in 1871, county cricket competitions began in 1873 and in 1877 the first tennis championships were held at Wimbledon. School teachers believed that organised games improved their pupils' characters.

> Manly sports played as they should be played tend to develop unselfish pluck, determination, self control and public spirit. Observe a group of School Board cricketers. No one quarrels with the placing of the field, they have learned to play the game.
>
> Quoted in P. Bailey, *Leisure and Class in Victorian England*, 1978

Parents in Brighton wrote in 1882 to those in charge of the Board Schools to suggest another reason for games.

> It is surely possible that some among the many who take an interest in the young would be glad to give a few hours on Saturday afternoons for the purpose of arranging a game of football. As things now are a section of the disbanded army of youngsters prowls about the streets eating rotting fruit and doing themselves no good in any way.
>
> Brighton School Board, 1882

But ordinary children could not usually afford equipment needed for games. Flora Thompson remembered the games enjoyed by village children.

> Marbles, pegtops and skipping ropes appeared in their season and where there happened to be a ball available a game called 'Tipit' was played. There was not always a ball to be had, for the smallest rubber one cost a penny and pennies were scarce. Even marbles at 20 a penny were seldom bought.
>
> *Lark Rise to Candleford*, 1945

Modern leather footballs were first manufactured in the 1870s. But the nearest many boys came to owning one was to wait till autumn, for

> in November came pig-killing time—soon our ears would be tormented with the screams of the expiring pig; then the pig was washed and cleaned. As children we hung round waiting for the bladder which when drained we blew up with a clay pipe stem and then used for a football.
>
> Quoted in I. Stickland, *Voices of Children*, 1973

Organised exercise became popular for girls too. In 1895 a magazine called *The Girls' Home Companion* reported,

Our girls have welcomed new outdoor sports and taken to many new indoor pastimes. Lawn tennis has apparently reached its maximum. Croquet, which was once out of fashion, seems to be reviving. Golf, one of the oldest games, has made a sudden leap into popularity and no book on pastimes would be complete on these days without an article on Cycling. Even cricket is now deemed suitable for girls.

Sometimes the effort to take exercise got people into trouble. In 1866 the *Bolton Chronicle* reported a trial where a Mr Wright was giving evidence.

On Saturday afternoon about half past two he was in his garden when he heard a noise in the road and turning round he saw a man pass by wearing nothing except a pair of drawers, while directly afterwards he saw the defendant running along the road in a completely nude state with the exception of a handkerchief which was wrapped around the loins. Witness added that he had been very much annoyed by this sort of thing lately. Defendant said he was only running for exercise.

1 Look at Picture 110. In what ways are the tennis players' clothes different from those worn today?
2 Why do you think female tennis players used to dress like this?
3 The Bolton runner was found guilty. Imagine you are the magistrate who is punishing him. Make up a speech telling him why his behaviour is wrong.

At the seaside

The railways made it easy for ordinary people (if they had enough money) to visit the seaside. In 1820 it took six hours to bump along from London to Brighton on top of a stagecoach.

111 Hastings (about 1888)

The fare was twelve shillings. Forty years later the train service took less than half the time. The fare was eight shillings. Around the coast seaside towns grew in size.

Some people went to the seaside just for the day. Factories organised outings like this one reported in a Blackburn paper.

> Fares were a shilling there and back. A band was provided by Messrs Hopwood and 200 loaves and from two to three hundredweight of cheese was stored in the horsebox.

This sort of day trip was the highlight of the year for many people. It was their one escape from their home town to a different place where they were free from the cares of home and work. Alfred Williams, who worked in Swindon, noticed that on the walls of the factory

> 'Roll on Trip' or 'Five Weeks to Trip' may be seen scrawled in big letters. 'Trip Day' is the most important day in the calendar at the railway town. For several months fathers and mothers, young men and juveniles have been saving up for the outing, whatever new clothes are bought for the summer are usually worn for the first time at 'Trip'.
>
> *Life in a Railway Factory*, 1915

Between 1863 and 1873 the numbers arriving by train at Blackpool Station increased four times. The town began to provide organised entertainments. In 1863 its North Pier was built for £13,500. In 1896 a gigantic wheel was put up. Growing numbers of these visitors came to stay for several days. Many seaside hotels were built in Victorian times though most visitors probably stayed in rented rooms in lodging houses. In some of these, people cooked their own meals. In others the landlady cooked food bought by the visitors.

Landladies were the target of jokes and criticisms. Writing in 1862 Robert Green saw them as either vultures or crocodiles,

> The first is generally at the top of the staircase ready to pounce upon the newcomer, while the latter usually ensconces [places] herself behind the flowerpots in the parlour, gazing with longing looks at the passers-by. She feeds her helps out of your larder and she makes the tradesmen give her a percentage for her recommendation. She attempts to make you pay for her butcher's bill.

Robert Green also stayed at lodgings where the landlady cooked all the meals. He did not enjoy his dinner.

> I take two spoonfuls of soup and find that it resembles a mixture of warm table beer thoroughly peppered. A piece of mutton streaking my plate with carmine, is now at my

112 *Dinner at a Brighton boarding house (1862)*

disposal, but I deem that eating raw mutton is simply eating raw sheep without the benefit of the wool to comfort your insides. I helped myself to a dish before me but to this day I am not certain of its composition.

Quoted in J. Anderson and E. Swinglehurst,
The Victorian and Edwardian Seaside, 1978

Landladies charged extra for doing washing and providing milk. Some charged for putting salt, pepper and sauce on the table. They also made money from day-trippers who came to the door for hot water. Writing in *The Rochdale Observer* Trafford Clegg joked about how a landlady packed in visitors.

Plenty of room, gentlemen, I have often had thirty people sleeping in the house and never more than seven in a bed. The parlour table holds five. Last summer I fitted a board over the scullery sink for two youngsters to sleep on and a hammock in the cellar steps with a breadth of carpet, and the clothes line. It was the coolest place in the house so I charged sixpence extra.

Quoted in J. K. Walton, *The Blackpool Landlady*, 1978

By the 1860s Britain's summer beaches were crowded. Brighton and Margate, according to Elizabeth Stone, were

crammed, but by decidedly unfashionable people. Look at these sands. They appear one moving mass of cabs, carts and carriages, horses, ponies, dogs, donkeys and boys; men, women, children and nurses, babies and bathing machines, little boys with spades, mamas with sewing and young ladies reading novels, young gentlemen with canes and eyeglasses. Then the hawkers [salesmen] are a most noisy and pressing fraternity here, nothing in the world that you can't buy from a puppy dog to a yard of cushion lace.

Chronicles of Fashion, 1845

113 *'Down at the seaside'*

The *Yarmouth Guide* of 1877 warned visitors to beware of salesmen on the beach.

> Take a seat and your troubles begin. 'Here's your chocolate creams.' 'Buns two a penny.' 'Yarmouth rock a penny a bar.' 'Apples penny a bag.' 'Nuts or pears.' 'Lemonade threepence a bottle.' 'Buy a bunch of grapes, Sir.' 'Walnuts eight a penny.' 'Milk a penny a glass.'

Bathing was popular, but men and women were strictly separated and had to use different parts of the beach. Women, in particular, went into the sea from 'bathing machines'. When William Tayler went to Brighton with his employers he saw some of these machines.

> There are numbers of old women have little wooden houses on wheeles, and into these houses people goe that want to bathe, and then the house is pushed into the water and when the person has undressed, they get into the water and bathe, and then get into the wooden house again and dress themselves, and then the house is drawn on shore again.
>
> Quoted in *Useful Toil*, 1974

Women wore a large quantity of heavy clothing when they went bathing. Many men wore nothing at all. In Victorian times seaside towns tried to persuade men to wear swimming costumes. In 1873 the Reverend Francis Kilvert was given special swimming clothes for the first time.

> At Seaton I had a bathe. A boy brought me to the machine door two towels, as I thought, but when I came out of the water and began to use them I found that one of the rags he had given me was a pair of very short red and white striped drawers to cover my nakedness. Unaccustomed to such things I had in my ignorance bathed naked and scandalised the beach. However some little boys who were looking on at the rude naked man appeared to be much interested in the spectacle and the young ladies who were strolling near seemed to have no objection.

In the following year Kilvert was persuaded—like more and more Victorians—to wear a swimming costume.

> At Shanklin one has to adopt the detestable custom of bathing in drawers. If ladies don't like to see men naked why don't they keep away from the sight? Today I had a

114 'Snobs at the seaside'

pair of drawers given me which I could not keep on. The rough waves stripped them off and tore them down round my ankles. I took the wretched and dangerous things off and of course there were some ladies looking on as I came up out of the water.

Kilvert's Diary, 1870–79, 1944

1 Name two ways in which a landlady could make extra money from visitors.
2 What do you think the menu for Robert Green's dinner might have looked like?
3 Design a sign to put outside your seaside lodging house to tempt in visitors.
4 Draw a holiday poster to advertise Hastings. Put a sketch of a bathing machine on the poster.
5 List at least three ways of spending time on a beach, as shown in Picture 113.
6 How many different things for sale are mentioned in the quotations? Is anything not mentioned that you would expect to find on a modern beach?
7 Design a notice to be put up near ladies' bathing machines warning people of all the rules and regulations for that part of the beach.

Sources and Acknowledgements

Thanks are due for permission to quote from copyright printed sources, and to the owners listed below for permitting the reproduction of illustrations.

Books

Abraham, J. J., *Harley Street and its Significance* (1926)

Adburgham, Alison, *Shops and Shopping* (London: George Allen & Unwin, 1964)

Anderson, J. and Swinglehurst, E., *The Victorian and Edwardian Seaside* (London: Country Life, 1978)

Archer, T., *The Pauper, the Thief and the Convict* (London: Groombridge & Sons, 1865)

Avery, G., *Victorian People in Life and in Literature* (London: Collins, 1970)

Bailey, P., *Leisure and Class in Victorian England* (London: Routledge & Kegan Paul, 1978)

Baring, M., *The Puppet Show of Memory* (London: Heinemann, 1922)

Barker, T. (ed.), *The Long March of Everyman* (London: BBC, 1975)

Beeton, I., *Book of Household Management* (1861; London: Jonathan Cape, 1968)

Benson, A. C. and Viscount Esher (eds), *Letters of Queen Victoria* (London: John Murray, 1905)

Blatchford, R., *My Life in the Army* (London: Clarendon Press, c. 1870; Daily Mail Sixpenny Novels, 1910)

Bobbitt, M. R. (ed.), *With Dearest Love to All: The Letters of Lady Jebb* (London: Faber, 1960)

Booth, C., *Life and Labour of the People in London*, 17 vols (London: Macmillan, 1889–1903)

Booth, W., *Darkest England and the Way Out* (London: Salvation Army, 1890)

Boyle, T., *Hope for the Canals!* (London: Simpkin, Marshall & Co., 1848)

Brewer, E. C., *My First Book of the History of England* (London: Cassell, 1864)

Brighton School Board, 1882

Burnett, J., *Plenty and Want* (London: Methuen, 1979)

Burnett, J., *Useful Toil* (London: Allen Lane, 1974)

Calder, J., *The Victorian Home* (London: B. T. Batsford, 1977)

Calthorpe, S. J. G., *Cadogan's Crimea* (1856; London: Hamish Hamilton, 1979)

Chance, W., *Children under the Poor Law* (Sonnenschein & Co., 1897)

Churchill, W. S., *My Early Life* (London: Thornton Butterworth, 1930)

Coghlan, F., *The Iron Road, Book and Railway Companion* (London: A. H. Baily & Co., 1838)

Coleman, T., *The Navvies* (Hutchinson, 1965)

Cook, T., *Jubilee Celebrations at Leicester and Market Harborough* (1886)

Cooper, Lady Diana, *The Rainbow Comes and Goes* (London: Rupert Hart-Davis, 1958)

Crow, D., *Victorian Women* (London: George Allen & Unwin, 1971)

Dawson, K. and Wall, P., *Public Health and Housing* (Oxford University Press, 1970)

Dixon, W. H., *London Prisons* (1850)

Dyos, H. J. and Wolff, M., *The Victorian City, Images and Reality* (London: Routledge & Kegan Paul, 1973)

Engels, F., *The Condition of the Working Class in England* (Leipzig, 1845)

Evans, L. and Pledger, P. J., *Contemporary Sources and Opinions in Modern British History*, 2 vols (London: Frederic Warne, 1967)

Farwell, B., *For Queen and Country* (London: Allen Lane, 1981)

Gaskell, Mrs E., *Life of Charlotte Brontë* (1857; Oxford University Press, 1961)

Gauldie, E., *Cruel Habitations* (London: George Allen & Unwin, 1974)

Goodman, M., *Experiences of an English Sister of Mercy* (London: 1862)

Gosden, P. H. J. H., *How They Were Taught* (Oxford: Basil Blackwell, 1969)

Graham, P. A., *The Rural Exodus: The Problems of the Village and the Town* (London: Methuen, 1892)

Greenwood, J., *A Night in a Workhouse* (Reprinted from the *Pall Mall Gazette*, 1866)

Haggard, H. Rider, *Rural England* (London: Longman, 1906)

Hartcup, A., *Below Stairs in Great Country Houses* (London: Sidgwick & Jackson, 1980)

Hawkes, J. (ed.), *The London Journal of Flora Tristan* (1842; London: Virago, 1982)

Head, F. O., *Stokers and Pokers, or the London and North Western Railway* (London: John Murray, 1849)

Heath, F. G., *The English Peasantry* (London, 1874)

Hewins, A. (ed.), *The Dillen* (Oxford University Press, 1982)

Higgs, M., *The Tramp Ward* (Manchester: reprinted from the Contemporary Review by John Haywood, 1904)

Hillyer, R., *Country Boy* (Sevenoaks: Hodder & Stoughton, 1966)

Historic Society of Lancashire and Cheshire (trans.), *Diary of John Ward of Clitheroe* (1953)

Hollis, C., *Eton* (London: Hollis & Co., 1960)

Horn, P., *Labouring Life in the Victorian Countryside* (London: Gill & Macmillan, 1976)

Howitt, W., *The Rural Life of England*, 2 vols (London: Longman, 1838)

Hughes, T., *Tom Brown's Schooldays* (London: Macmillan, 1857)

Jefferies, R., *Hodge and his Masters* (London: Smith, Elder & Co., 1880)

Jefferies, R., *The Toilers of the Field* (London: Longman, 1892)

Kingsley, F. E. (ed.), *Charles Kingsley: His Letters and Memories of his Life* (H. S. King, 1879)

Kitchen, F., *Brother to the Ox* (London: J. M. Dent, 1963)

Lancashire Record Office, 1842

Leach, R. A., *Pauper Children, their education and training, a complete handbook to the law* (London: Hadden, Best & Co., 1890)

Leader, R. E., *Life and Letters of J. A. Roebuck* (London: Edward Arnold, 1897)

Leifchild, J. R., *Our Coal and our Coal Pits, by a Traveller Underground* (London: Traveller's Library, 1853)

Longmate, N., *The Workhouse* (London: Temple Smith, 1974)

McLevy, James, *The Casebook of a Victorian Detective* (Edinburgh: Canongate, 1975)

Macmullen, J., *Camp and Barrack Room, or the British Army as it is* (London: Chapman & Hall, 1846)

Macqueen-Pope, W., *Give Me Yesterday* (London: Hutchinson, 1957)

'The Major of Today', *Clothes and the Man* (London: Grant Richards, 1900)

Mann, T., *Tom Mann's Memoirs* (London: Labour Publishing Co., 1923)

Manners and Rules of Good Society, anon. (1888)

Manton, J., *Elizabeth Garrett Anderson* (London: Methuen, 1965)

Mayhew, H., *London Labour and the London Poor* (1851; London: Frank Cass, 1967)

Mearns, A., *The Bitter Cry of Outcast London* (1883: Leicester University Press, 1970)

Millin, G. F., *Life in Our Villages by the Special Correspondent on The Daily News* (1891)

Mole, E., *A King's Hussar* (London: Cassell, 1893)

Morris, M. C., *Yorkshire Reminiscences* (Humphrey Milford, 1922)

Nightingale, F., *Notes on Hospitals* (London: J. W. Parker & Sons, 1865)

Nightingale, F., *Notes on Nursing* (London: Harrison & Sons, 1860)

Norfolk WI, *Within Living Memory* (1971)

Palmer, R., *A Touch on the Times* (Harmondsworth: Penguin, 1974)

Palmer, R., *The Rambling Soldier* (Harmondsworth: Penguin, 1977)

Parliamentary Papers, 1840 (vol. 11), 1842 (vols 15, 16, 26), 1843 (vols 13, 14, 15), 1844 (vol. 18), 1845 (vols 3, 18), 1847 (vol. 12), 1863 (vol. 18)

Parliamentary Debates, 1864, 1870

Perry, G. and Mason, N., *Rule Britannia* (Times Newspapers, 1974)

Pike, E. Royston, *Human Documents of the Age of the Forsytes* (London: George Allen & Unwin, 1969)

Plomer, W. (ed.), *Kilvert's Diary, 1870–79* (London: Cape, 1944)

Postgate, R., *A Life of George Lansbury* (London: Longman, 1951)

Prisons Act, 1898

Privy Council Medical Reports, 1866

Raverat, Gwen, *Period Piece* (London: Faber, 1952)

Report of the Army Sanitary Commission, 1857–8

Report of the Committee of the Council on Education, 1845; 1850–51

Report of the Select Committee on the Andover Workhouse, 1846

Robertson, W. R., *From Private to Field Marshall* (London: Constable, 1921)

Rose, W., *Good Neighbours* (1969)

Rowntree, B. S., *Poverty, a Study of Town Life* (London: Macmillan, 1901; New York: Howard Fertig, 1971)

Samuel, R. (ed.), *East End Underworld* (London: Routledge & Kegan Paul, 1981)

Samuel, R. (ed.), *Miners, Quarrymen and Salt Workers* (London: Routledge & Kegan Paul, 1977)

Sanger, G., *Seventy Years a Showman* (MacGibbon & Kee, 1966)

Sava, G. A., *Twice the Clock Round* (1859; London: Faber, 1940)

Scott-Giles, C. W., *The Road Goes On* (London: Epworth Press, 1946)

Sherard, R. H. *The White Slaves of England* (London: J. Rowden, 1897)

Sims, G. R., *How the Poor Live* (London: Chatto & Windus, 1883)

Sitwell, O., *The Scarlet Tree* (London: Macmillan, 1946)

Skelley, A. Ramsey, *The Victorian Army at Home* (London: Croom Helm, 1977)

Smith, A. R., *The Struggles and Adventures of Christopher Tadpole, at Home and Abroad* (London: 1848)

Smullen, I., *Taken for a Ride* (London: Jenkins, 1968)

Snow, J., *On the Mode of the Communication of Cholera* (1849; new ed. London, 1855)

Somerville, A., *The Autobiography of a Working Man* (1848; Wellingborough: Turnstone Press, 1951)

Sproule, A., *The Social Calendar* (Poole: Blandford Press, 1978)

Stickland, I., *Voices of Children, 1700–1914* (Oxford: Basil Blackwell, 1973)

Stone, E., *Chronicles of Fashion* (London: 1845)

Sykes, J., *Slawit in the Sixties* (London: Schofield & Sims, 1926)

Taine, H. A., *Notes on England* (reprinted in the *Daily News*, 1872)

Thompson, Flora, *Lark Rise to Candleford* (Oxford University Press, 1945)

Thorndike, A. R., *Children of the Garter* (Rich & Cowan, 1937)

Tobias, J. J., *Nineteenth-Century Crime: Prevention and Punishment* (Newton Abbot: David & Charles, 1972)

Walker, C., *Thomas Brassey, Railway Builder* (London: Frederick Muller, 1969)

Walton, J. K., *The Blackpool Landlady* (Manchester University Press, 1978)

Walvin, J., *Leisure and Society, 1850–1950* (London: Longman, 1978)

Wilkes, J., *The London Police in the Nineteenth Century* (Cambridge University Press, 1977)

Williams, Alfred, *Life in a Railway Factory* (1915)

Woodham Smith, C., *Florence Nightingale* (London: Constable, 1950)

Newspapers and periodicals

Aylesbury News, 11 May 1839

The Bolton Chronicle, 7 March 1866

Chambers' *Edinburgh Journal*, 1856

The Cornhill Magazine, 1862, May 1874

Daily News, 1872, 1891

Daily Telegraph, 1865

Edinburgh Review, April 1963

The Girls' Home Companion, 1895

The Globe, 1863

The Illustrated London News, 1850

The Illustrated Police News, 8 September 1888

The Morning Chronicle, 1848–50, 1886

The New Sporting Magazine

The Quarterly Review, 1867

The Times, 5 July 1849, 15 November 1864, August 1871, 3 April 1883, 19 October 1961

Illustrations

1, 3, 7, 11, 17, 32, 33, 35, 36, 38, 40, 41, 42, 50, 56, 63, 64, 69, 75, 85, 86, 88, 89, 103, 104, 109, BBC Hulton Picture Library; 2, 25, 26, 27, 28, 29, 34, 61, 67, 70, 78, 93, The Illustrated London News Picture Library; 4, reproduced by gracious permission of Her Majesty Queen Elizabeth II; 5, 9, 10, 18, 19, 21, 23, 30, 31, 43, 54, 66, 71, 73, 84, 94, 105, Mary Evans Picture Library; 6, 8, 22, Royal Commission on Historical Monuments (England); 12, 52, 57, 92, 95, 96, 110, 114, Punch Publications Limited; 13, 24, 91, 102, 107, 108, The Mansell Collection; 14, Popperfoto; 15, from M. Girouard, *Life in the English Country House*; 16, University Library, Cambridge; 20, 45, 47, 48, 49, 51, Institute of Agricultural History and Museum of English Rural Life, University of Reading; 37, The Mitchell Library, Glasgow; 39, British Museum; 44, 46, City of Birmingham Reference Library; 53, 82, 99, Guildhall Library, London; 55, N. B. Traction, Dundee; 58, Strathclyde Regional Council; 59, 80, 83, Aberdeen University; 60, 62, 65, 72, City of Aberdeen Library; 68, Beamish North of England Open Air Museum; 74, 111, John Topham Picture Library; 76, Ironbridge Gorge Museum Trust; 77, Leicester Museum; 79, Weidenfeld & Nicolson Archives; 81, S. A. Wood; 87, County Museum, Taunton; 97, 98, Police Staff College, Bramshill; 100, 101, Edinburgh City Libraries; 106, Raymond Mander and Joe Mitcherson Theatre Collection; 112, British Library; 113, Brighton Reference Library.